Addys Boston

The author - 1987

FROM THE FENS TO WESTMINSTER AND BACK

OR

WHAT PRICE INDEPENDENCE

By

Hilda Clarke

1988

RICHARD KAY

80 SLEAFORD ROAD, BOSTON, LINCOLNSHIRE PE21 8EU

ISBN 0 902662 77 5 cased edition
ISBN 0 902662 78 3 paperback edition

CONTENTS

ILLUSTRATIONS

For more than fifty years the camera, the holiday snapshot, the family album, and the collection of miscellaneous pictures have become commonplace in many households. Without the gift of sight, however, pictures have a much diminished personal significance and, even if collected, cannot always be identified. For these reasons little illustrative material has been availiable and even less has been suitable for inclusion in this book.

In addition to the frontispiece those that have been included may be found between pages 26 & 27 and between pages 106 & 107.

ACKNOWLEDGEMENTS

We are grateful to Mr. D. A. Heald for permission to reproduce his drawing of Kings Manor, York and to Addys of Boston for permission to reproduce the frontispiece portrait.

INTRODUCTION

The story which I am about to unfold might be compared with a patchwork quilt. Like a quilt it varies greatly from patch to patch. Some parts are bright and colourful while other parts may appear to be rather drab and uninteresting. Since I am blind and have no idea of colours I am not able to describe the variations in shades. For the first few years of my life I could detect daylight from darkness. Therefore I think of colours as being either dark or light. I could not see objects. This may have accounted for my many pitfalls. The small glimmer of sight I possessed in early life has faded with the years. All that remains is a white mist whether day or night. I understand that other people are similarly placed, and that the condition is known as white blindness. As a child I knew nothing of this, nor that there was any difference between me and the rest of my family.

In the following pages I shall try to put on record some of my experiences and relationships between family and friends.

To Helen Fenning

With my grateful thanks for her
encouragement and interest in this
book, and for giving so
generously of her time in helping
at all stages of its preparation.

1.

IN THE EARLY DAYS

It was Tuesday, 9 April 1913, my sixth birthday. This day stands out in my memory. It was a very warm spring day and late afternoon. As usual on warm days the kitchen door stood open to the gravel yard with a row of elderberry bushes along the right side, and along the left side there were the usual outhouses. Then, at the far end of the yard opposite the kitchen door, there was a deep dyke which was fenced right along with wire meshing. To the right of this fence there was a narrow bridge with a rail on both sides over the dyke which led to a cinder track road. The small gate to this bridge was always kept fastened for safety reasons. To the right of the kitchen door was a concrete path which led down to a long garden with a pig sty at the very far end. The sun streamed in through the open kitchen door. I sat on the broad white doorstep in the warm sunshine. Facing me on the kitchen wall I could see the thin strands of sunlight reaching down like fingers, each finger ending in a point. This pattern made by the sun intrigued me when I was younger, and I remember trying to scratch off the wall the bright streaks of sunshine with my fingernails much to my mother's annoyance at my marking the wall.

Many were the hours I spent sitting on this doorstep dressing and undressing my rag dolls. This being my birthday I had been given a new rag doll, this one dressed in doll's clothes, not the odd pieces of material from my mother's workbasket. This doll had a china head with hair. It didn't have eyes that opened and closed as they do today. It wore white socks and shoes. This was the best and largest doll I had ever received from anyone. Obviously someone had dressed it for me. In those days there wasn't much money to be spent on toys. Imagination played a great part in our amusement.

There was the clink of plates and pots and pans coming from

the kitchen where my mother was preparing the evening meal. We all had our hot meal of the day when my father came home from work about 5.00 p.m. We sat round the large square table in the centre of the kitchen with its starched white cloth. The meal was cooked on the kitchen range. The dishes were placed on the bright steel fender to be kept hot. The black shiny kettle hung on a hook immediately above the fire. The meal sometimes consisted of cabbage and boiled bacon, home cured from our own pig, reared and fed by my father. All the vegetables were from our garden which was also tended by my father. He would sometimes let me help him with the weeding until I pulled up all his onions by mistake. In those days it was the custom to eat the sweet dish before the meat course. Quite often it would be boiled pudding with fruit from the garden in season, or in winter with jam, treacle, or brown sugar and vinegar. Then of course there were the various milk puddings. My favourite was baked rice done in the side oven for hours. Then on Sundays we had roast beef and Yorkshire pudding. On Mondays we had the beef cold, with pickles and chutneys which my mother had made. The butcher called only on Saturdays in those isolated areas. My father often shot a rabbit during the winter months and mother made some very tasty meals from it. We had rabbit pies or rabbit stewed with plenty of good broth with dumplings.

On the fine warm evenings after our meal we were sent out of doors to play awhile until time for bed. More often than not when it came to bedtime I was not ready and would do all I could to delay as long as possible. Then my mother would get cross. Many were the times I was sent to bed in tears on summer evenings. But this was my birthday. I could stay up a little longer. I was interested in playing with the new ball my father had bought for me and had painted white so that I might be able to see it. Whenever they gave me a new ball my father painted it white as I am sure he really believed I could see it, but I couldn't. Sooner or later I lost them all. However this ball stands out in my memory. It turned out that it was the last one my father ever painted white for me. I didn't have it very long before it rolled into the muddy dyke at the top of the garden.

At that time there were four of us children in the family. I was the eldest; then there was a brother, Harry, five years of age, who was also blind and amused himself all day playing at engines.

2

He was my mother's pet. I don't remember him getting into any scrapes.

Next, there was Ethel, aged three, who spent quite a lot of her time with Gran and Grandad who lived about three miles away. Often during weekends and holidays when the weather was good my parents took us to see Gran and Grandad. I thought it seemed a very long walk. The country roads in those days were very lonely. Perhaps one would meet an old motorcar or, during the week, the horse-drawn vehicles and farm machines, and the odd bicycle. Though I quite enjoyed visiting my grandparents I wasn't too keen about staying there with them. I did stay with them when I was younger and made such a fuss to go home that my father had to be sent for to take me home one evening after a hard day's work. I remember riding on the seat at the back of his bicycle.

I did love my Gran, she was a super old lady, but my Grandad was so particular about his garden. I must not touch anything or walk on the onions, peas, or beans or go near the dog or leave the gate open. It was 'don'ts' all the time. Grandad's roses were his pride and joy; there were climbing ones all over the front of the house, and bush roses along the edge of the garden. As he didn't like to see me touch them I had to look at them when he had gone out for his walk or was having his afternoon rest. I liked to feel the velvety blooms and to this day I remember the beautiful perfume. I discovered that the roses climbing along the front of the house were called tea roses. Their perfume wasn't quite so strong but just a sweet fresh smell and they were much smaller than the bush roses. Then there were the Canterbury Bells. When I first felt these they reminded me of a cup and saucer. They were fairly large, and so far as I remember gave off very little perfume, if any. I never knew their colour. I think I liked the sweet peas best. They have the loveliest perfume; the curved petals remind me of small wings. These occasional visits to my grandparents made a nice change for we never went away for holidays in those days. My parents never had a holiday as far as I know.

The fourth and youngest member of our family was Mabel, fourteen months old at that time. My memories of her are that she was screaming most of the time. I sat for many long hours rocking her cradle in the chimney corner, but she seldom slept. I would sit on the floor beside the cradle singing to her making up the words as I sang. This was indeed a very boring task. In the end I usually sneaked away to find more interesting things to do outside. I would get as far away from the house as possible out of earshot should my mother call me to do more rocking. Very rarely would I sit just doing nothing. Nor do I remember ever feeling lonely. I always liked my own company and still do. On summer days I liked to sit on the grassy patch behind the elderberry bushes in the shade. Here I would make daisy chains. I can't remember playing with my brother very often; he was too busy playing at engines. At the time we had a black cat which would allow me to do anything I liked with him. I remember dressing him up in the baby's dress and decorating him with daisy-chains. Quite often my mother would appear, no doubt to see what I was doing, and she retrieved the baby's dress and banished the cat. I am afraid he did not enjoy many home comforts for my father didn't like him in the house. He would say a cat's place was in the yard catching mice. I think the cat knew the house was out of bounds as he didn't attempt to go inside unless I carried him in on the quiet when nobody else was around.

The summer of 1913 was quite an eventful one as far as I was concerned. Mr. H. Carter, my father's boss, had advised my parents to take me to Moorfields Eye Hospital in London to see an eye specialist and he would pay all the expenses. All the aunts and uncles who visited us felt that something should be done about my eyes. That is how I knew I had bad eyes. I became the object of interest and arrangements were soon in hand for me to see a specialist. Letters arrived quite frequently. In the remote areas the postmen either had to walk or cycle down long cinder-track roads. Sometimes during bad winters our mail was left at the farm house for my father to collect.

The evening before my trip to London my mother told me that I would have to be up early the next morning and that I would be riding in a train. The tin bath was brought into the kitchen and placed on the hearth-rug in front of the fire. It was filled with hot water drawn from the boiler attached to the kitchen range. I was duly bathed and my hair washed and rolled into ringlets by twisting the hair round strips of rag tied at the end of each ringlet. My mother often curled my hair in this way at weekends if we were going out. I had very fine hair which was almost white at that time. I remember having to listen to my mother's usual lectures before going out anywhere about not forgetting to say "please" and "thank you". The same advice was meted out when we had visitors.

The next morning I was aroused from my bed very early. Dressed in my Sunday dress, coat, and hat, I was strapped in the seat at the back of my father's bicycle. We were on our way to Littleworth station. On arrival we were soon aboard the London train. This was the first time I had ridden in a train. How excited I was! This was indeed a new experience for me. I wandered round the compartment examining anything I could find and asking questions. My father wiped my dirty fingers on his large white handkerchief many times. The carriage was crowded, the people spoke to me and I wasn't at all shy of strangers. My father insisted that I should sit down beside him for a while though I don't remember how long. In those days I never sat down quietly for very long. In my wanderings round the carriage I encountered the window blinds. I had never seen anything like them before. I was fascinated by the way they shot up and down by simply pulling a cord. Again my father put an end to all this and once more wiped my dirty fingers on his handkerchief. There were no washing facilities on most of the trains in those days. They were very, very dirty with the smoke from the engine. As we reached the tunnels approaching King's Cross people closed the windows to keep out the engine smoke. The one thing I remember about the tunnels is that I was afraid of the noise and the horrid smell. This train journey is quite fresh in my memory today. I certainly learned a lot from my own observations and from the answers to all my questions. My father possessed much more patience than my mother; she was always too busy and just sent me out of the way.

At last we arrived at King's Cross. Again the noise and the crowds worried me. I had never been so afraid, and remember thinking I would lose my father in these pushing crowds. This dislike of large crowds has stayed with me even to this day. My father carried me down endless flights of stairs to the tube. He was probably familiar with the tubes as he had served in the army when young and travelled abroad quite a lot. We boarded the tube train. I heard the doors slide to close. I noticed the stale smell of the tunnels again as we rode to our destination. This train was very crowded and we had to stand for a short time. I remember holding tight to my father's hand for fear of getting lost. This journey is well stamped on my mind and I have lived it again and again in my dreams. I have this recurring dream of being lost in a crowd and nobody wants to know. What a relief to wake up and feel safe again! The time came for us to leave the tube train and I learned afterwards that we were heading for Moorfields Eye Hospital. After a few enquiries by my father we did eventually arrive there. I was most fascinated by it all. Everybody wore white and the whole place was white and bright. Someone, I suppose it was a nurse, took hold of my hand and led us into a large room which sounded to be full of people. I could hear the clink of crockery. I remember we were given a cup of tea and somebody in white washed my face and hands. I was made a fuss of and given a bag of sweets. Then a nurse took us into a small room where we were kept waiting ages for the doctor. I remember sitting upon someone's knee and the doctor pulling my eyes open and shining into them a bright light. Some cool drops were put into them and I didn't like that at all. However, after what appeared to be a very long time, the doctor talked to my father. We were then shown out of the hospital.

The thing that struck me most about the hospital was that it was so very hot and my father, who couldn't stand a lot of heat, was very pleased to get out into the fresh air again. I didn't know how the examination had gone at the hospital but on the train going home my father told me that I would have to wear glasses, and that I must not rush about so much until I had got used to wearing them. He also told me that my eyes would get better as I grew older and stronger. The day's excitement had made me tired and I slept most of the return journey home. Nevertheless, I had enjoyed all the attention given me by the doctors and nurses. We arrived home where my mother was pleased to see us. This had been the longest outing I had ever experienced. What a lot I had to tell my mother about the trip to London. I never stopped talking until my mother told me to be quiet!

A few days later my glasses arrived as prescribed by the specialist. In spite of all my protests I was made to wear them. I didn't like them at all. They were most uncomfortable around my ears. I had to wear them until bedtime. However, as the time passed, the glasses proved to be not much of a success. About every other day in my rushing around I managed to crash into something and break them. I always managed to break them on wash days by banging into the clothes props. I would bang into trees and into brick walls. I just couldn't see any more with them than I could without them. In the end my father became rather fed up with having to cycle into Spalding nearly every evening after work to have the glasses repaired, and the idea of my wearing glasses was abandoned.

On a scorching hot day in July 1913 I was sitting in my favourite spot on the kitchen doorstep listening to my parents talking. I heard something interesting. My father had been offered a new job as farm foreman. We were to move to a new house in October. I was very excited but of course I did not understand how long it would be until October. So when I asked my father he told me we would not be moving until after the harvest. This news gave me something to think about while sitting on the doorstep with my dolls and the pieces of material I pretended were dresses and underclothes, all from my mother's work-basket. From a very early age I had longed for a work-basket of my own. This didn't come until much later. I was never allowed scissors and no matter how long I looked I could never find any.

I had a very unpleasant experience one day when I climbed upon the arm of a chair to see what I would find in the work-basket which stood on a shelf in the corner. I lost my balance and fell down into the corner dragging down with me work-basket, shelf, and everything else. I was immediately sent to bed as a punishment. However, everything was alright in the morning. I was also interested in odd pieces of wool and collected all the bits my aunt could spare. My mother taught me how to make a chain with one loop on a meat skewer. I wasn't allowed knitting needles as it was thought that I might stick them into my eyes. The points were cut off the skewers. I did manage to make chains with the skewers and odd pieces of wool. This simple task occupied me for hours. During summer evenings my father spent much of his time in the garden. I would be there following him around until I was called indoors for bed. It was always with reluctance I had to yield to my mother in the end.

Whatever other folk were doing I also had to be busy. Friday was my mother's baking day. I would be there in the kitchen and to keep me out of the way my mother would give me a piece of the dough which I would roll out with a clothes peg into all shapes and sizes. I saw to it that this went into the oven to be baked with the rest. "It doesn't look very appetising" my mother often

7

said as she threw it out on to the rack. But I had made it and I was proud of it. I have to admit that it was rather hard and tasteless but the pigs ate it. My mother sometimes made some of our bread. I still remember the large bowl of dough standing on the kitchen fender to rise, covered with a large cloth. This large mountain of dough rose well above the rim of the bowl. The smell of home-made bread lingered about the house for a long time. The pantry shelves were piled up with jam and lemon curd tarts, mince pies, and egg custards, all cooling on wire racks. After baking the large wooden table had to be scrubbed and the kitchen floor washed. How my mother worked in those days! Then there were wash-days and I also had a hand in them somewhere. I was given my own bowl of water to wash the pieces of material which were my doll's clothes. I used to hang them on the elderberry bushes to dry. Messing about with water was a favourite with me and would amuse me for hours. Nobody seemed to mind as long as I was out of the way.

However, at last it was October and the move to our new house drew nearer. Packing and dismantling were going ahead during the evenings. My father must have been a most patient man for he had to answer the many questions I posed. I gathered that the new home was larger than the one we now occupied. There were no dykes immediately close to the house as there were in our present abode. My mother had rescued me so many times from the ones close to our present house. On reflection the thing that struck me most was the fact that I had got my clean clothes dirty and had to be bathed - not the fact that I might have been drowned, for the dyke close to the house was very deep, especially in winter. I know I fell into this dyke three times. The memory of this frightened me for years, and I had nightmares until I was much older, but they disappeared after I learned how to swim at school.

The preparation for the move progressed. All the pictures had been taken down, shelves and fittings removed. I don't remember carpets except the stair carpet and loose rugs. How the house echoed with the floor coverings taken up!

We now come to our last evening in the old house on Carter's farm. We children were sent to bed very early. The two paraffin lamps were taken down and packed. When darkness came candles had to be used. The last of the packing was finished.

8

Next morning we were all up and dressed just after daylight. Breakfast completed, the beds were taken down and packed. All the furniture and belongings were stacked on two farm wagons loaned to us by a neighbouring farmer. Here were my mother, father, and us children sitting in the front surrounded by cardboard boxes, cases, crockery, and glassware, father's bicycle, baby's pram, and goodness knows what. Nobody could find the cat. I often wonder what happened to him.

We were on our way to the new house on Earl's farm in Counterdrain which was as isolated as the one we were leaving. A new era was in front of us. What did the future hold in store?

2.

THE NEW HOME

The removal to the new house proceeded according to plan. All the painting and decorating had been completed. We all settled down to the daily routine on the farm. There were four bedrooms, two of which were fairly large, a sitting-room, a kitchen, and a very large pantry or dairy. My sister and I shared the bedroom above the kitchen. This was said to be the warmest bedroom because of the heat from the kitchen range. But I wonder! For during the very sharp winters there was ice inside and the window so frozen it couldn't be opened. When the north winds blew the door rattled and had to be wedged. In fact it was a common occurrence for the draught to blow out the candle on the top stair - placed there while we undressed. The younger ones were scared in the dark. There was no electricity or gas so the only source of lighting was a candle and downstairs a paraffin lamp hung from the ceiling. As we were at war the windows were blacked out by a thick blind and curtain.

When I was young the winters were always cold and frosty and the snow seemed to hang about for months.

I learned my way about fairly quickly as I followed my father around. We certainly lived in a very isolated area. Our nearest neighbour lived about twenty minutes' walk away. There were two roads by which we could leave the farm. We could walk across two grass fields and cross over a dyke by a narrow plank which brought us up to a long lonely road leading into Spalding. It was called Cuckoo Road. The other route into town was by way of a cinder track to Counterdrain station. This was the route the tradesmen took. In those days it was mostly horse and trap, although some farmers did possess motor cars. This cinder track used to be very muddy during the wet weather in winter. There was a dyke for part of the way on one side. It took about twenty minutes to walk to the station. There were five trains each way every day except Sundays. We were fairly well served by the tradesfolk of Spalding. James the baker and Adams the butcher called twice a week, and Billetts the grocer once a week. If the roads were snarled up with snow they would leave their goods at the station with the stationmaster, and my father had to walk to the station to collect them. He had a very rough journey sometimes when the weather was bad. Every morning my father collected the daily paper and our mail, if there was any, from the station.

On Saturday afternoons my mother would take the three o'clock train into Spalding to go shopping. The journey took about ten minutes. She would return by the six o'clock train. When the weather was bad my father made the trip. Shopping wasn't much in his line and he usually forgot something important.

There was no problem with our milk because my father had the use of a cow. He milked it twice daily. My mother skimmed off the cream for making butter, some of which went to Mr. T. A. White, my father's boss. As the cream was taken off the milk each day it was stored in large pancheons. It was stirred regularly. On Thursdays it was put into a large wooden churn. Somebody had the boring task of turning the handle until the butter was made. This could take hours especially if the day was a cold one. I often had to sit on a stool and turn the handle. When the weather was very cold and the butter just wouldn't come, I have known my mother put a little hot water into the churn. This did speed up things and it was a grand sound to hear the liquid splashing around and the butter knocking against the sides. My mother could see when the butter had arrived through a glass panel in the front of the churn. This stage completed, the next was making up the butter into pounds. Each piece was weighed and knocked into shape with two flat pieces of wood with a handle at one end. These were about six inches long and three inches wide and were called clappers. One side was patterned and this made the butter look attractive. Each pound was pressed into shape with the clappers. This was done on the long marble slab in the pantry or dairy. When set it was wrapped in greaseproof paper which had been cut out for the job. The dairy was cold enough to keep the food fresh all the time. There was a long safe with wire mesh doors down one side, and all food, including joints of meat, could be stored. We never went hungry although it was wartime and so much food was on

11

ration. My father's wages were thirty-six shillings a week. We paid no rent, we had our milk, butter, and any eggs we needed. These perks must have been a great help. The young wagoner, or horsekeeper as we called him, was boarded with us and he paid fourteen shillings a week. My mother made most of our clothes and knitted stockings and gloves, etc. We must have been better off than our friends living in town.

Our day started at five in the morning when the wagoner would be up and out in the stable feeding and harnessing the horses which might be needed for the day's work on the farm. Then again in the evening he spent more time in the stable feeding and grooming the horses and turning them into the stable yard for the night during the winter. During the summer after their supper they were turned into the grass field for the night. Although I was rather afraid of the big horses I did like them and knew all their names. Much against my mother's wishes I often crept into the small building adjoining the stable called the gear house where the harnesses hung. The wagoner used to polish the brasses on the harness. It hung on pegs all round the gear house wall. The food for the horses was also kept in this building. I remember the large bins of corn and chaff and the sack of locust standing in one corner. This had a lovely smell and was very sweet to eat. I loved to hear the wagoner scoop the corn and chaff and toss them into the manger where the horses soon pounced on them. The horses stood in a row, all chained to the manger, while they were feeding. They were all called by their names - Lightfoot, Rattler, Bouncer, Punch, Flower, Sharper, and Soldier. I have never forgotten them. How thrilled I was when one morning my father told me that Flower had got a foal. I didn't let him have any peace until he let me touch it. But, alas, when it got bigger it had to go to market.

Really the yard was out of bounds when the horses were working. Nevertheless I'm afraid these rules were not always adhered to. I found the farmyard rather fascinating and liked to wander round the various buildings, especially the barn when the men were cutting chaff for the horses. This was done by a small engine attached to the chaff-cutting box by a belt. It ran on petrol and chuffed and hummed. This was just what my brother loved for his great interest was engines. The chaff piled up in a huge bin. Large bundles of straw were placed in the chaff-box, and as it ran through the knives one could hear the chaff rolling into the bins. On the whole it was a noisy operation. I was very scared of noise and kept at a distance. Cattle cake and corn were stored in the barn. Adjoining the barn was the steam house. In here were two tall steamers below which were two small fire grates to heat the water to boil the potatoes for the pigs and, during the winter, the chickens. They were looked after by Norman, the odd job boy on the farm. One whole sack of potatoes went into each steamer at a time. Before being tipped into the steamers the potatoes went through a machine to be washed. I had a go at turning the handle. The place used to get full of steam but we did not bother, and as soon as the potatoes were cooked and Norman had turned them out into a bin by tilting the steamers to empty them, we loved to have one put aside to cool so that we could eat it. I have never enjoyed boiled potatoes in their skins so much. This was only on cold days for we did not boil potatoes during the summer months: then they were given raw.

In the early days on the farm, during the war, the pig-sties and the cattle-yards were full of animals which were sent to market in the spring. I can remember in early summer how the place smelled while the workmen were carting and spreading the manure over all the fields for fertilisation purposes. The animals were watered by means of a trough in their yards filled from pipes attached to a pump in the stable yard a little distance away. These pipes had to be rigged up for the purpose and then dismantled when the water tank was full. This was Norman's job. It was a seven-day-a-week task. Even on Sundays somebody had to work a couple of hours to fill the tanks. Of all the creatures on the farm, Joey, the cockerel, was the most frightening as far as I was concerned. His crow was so loud, and he could be quite nasty too. On one occasion he knocked my small sister over and stole the piece of cake she was eating out of her hand. He even stole from the kitchen table one afternoon. He was around for a long time.

On occasions I went round with my father looking for the eggs which the hens seemed to lay all over. We found them under haystacks, in nesting boxes and hen houses, or under ploughs in the implement shed. It was quite usual in the summer to find a nest with several eggs in the cornfields. Years later we acquired a dog, Mick. He was a fox terrier, white with brown ears and a brown patch on one side, just as though someone had thrown a paint brush at him. When they were working in the yard during

13

the day he was kept chained to his kennel, which was close to the house, for fear that he might get in the way of the horses.   He wouldn't sleep in the house so went back into his kennel at night. During the winter prior to my starting school one hen dared to lay an egg in his kennel every day.   The hen approached the kennel. Without any fuss at all Mick would turn out, jump on top of the kennel, and stand there in the cold until the hen came out cackling while the dog barked furiously until someone retrieved the egg from the kennel. When I became older he accompanied me on walks, though he spent most of his time in the dykes ratting, and should we meet anyone coming along the road he would hasten to my side and stay there until the person had well passed us. He took a dislike to the postman, bit the baker, and growled at anyone he didn't like.

One morning in 1914 we sat round the kitchen table having lunch and, as so often, my father was reading the daily paper to my mother.   I heard him say that war had started. This was the chief topic of conversation between my parents for days.   I could hear them discussing matters from my bedroom above the kitchen. My father had received his calling up papers for war service. For days my mother seemed more anxious and more irritable than usual. My father did tell us that he might be going to be a soldier.   My mother's headaches became more frequent.   This meant I had better keep well out of her way.   My father would read the war news to my mother during the morning lunch break.   There were no radio sets in those days: the newspapers provided what information there was. Everybody anxiously awaited the local weekly paper which had the list of people missing or dead.   Some of my father's workers had been called up, including our wagoner.   He was only eighteen years of age when he enlisted for service in the forces. I remember the night he said his goodbye to us.   My parents had become very fond of him and treated him as one of the family. Some months later we heard from the local paper that he had been killed in action in France.   It was the first death in my life and I gave it quite a lot of thought.

The autumn and winter of 1914 saw changes on the farm. There were women working in the fields in place of the young men. During the winter German prisoners were employed to dig out the snow and do the land work. I think there must have been a prisoner-of-war camp not very far away.   They were in the charge of an

14

officer. They were brought in by horse and trolley every morning and returned to their camp every evening. They spent their meal breaks in the granary where there was a coke stove on which they boiled water for hot drinks. They brought their food with them for the day.

One morning during that winter my father received a letter by post telling him he was exempt from Army service. His boss had intervened for him because he was already performing a useful service to the community in agricultural work. I believe that was the usual practice with key men in agriculture. My mother must have been very relieved at this news. If he had gone to serve in the forces it might have altered the whole course of all our lives. We certainly couldn't have stayed on our own in that isolated spot.

We are now in 1915. The news is still about the war and soldiers missing and German submarines being sunk. I could hear my parents discussing things while I lay in bed in my room above the kitchen. There was a shortage of tea and sugar. My parents gave up sugar in their drinks in order that my mother could make jam and chutney. In our garden we only had blackcurrant bushes, though fruit was easily procured from neighbouring farms at reasonable prices. I can remember eating apples at sixpence a stone. Some cooking apples were much cheaper. Victoria plums were only a few pence a stone. Very often we had baskets of fruit given us. My mother complained about the flour and the bread being dark in colour. Sometimes after the harvest my father would have a sack of wheat ground into flour by the miller for our use. It was fine for making home-made bread or puddings. My father grew all the vegetables in season. We were fortunate in that we had a large greenhouse where we grew tomatoes and cucumbers during the summer months. During the winter potatoes for seed for the next year's crops were stored in chitting boxes. In winter when the sun shone this was the warmest spot on the farm. My parents worked very hard, especially my mother. As well as all the sewing, cooking, and cleaning, there was always a baby to attend to. The clothes line underneath the high mantlepiece in the kitchen was usually full of baby's nappies, etc., airing.

In early May 1915 we had a surprise. We had another addition to the family. My youngest brother was born. We were all dressed and about very early that morning. There seemed to be a lot of folk hanging around, my Aunt Emma, Gran, and a woman whose name I don't know. She didn't speak to me. I could hear her bustling about upstairs assisting my mother in making the beds, generally tidying up, and moving furniture about. The door which led upstairs was open. I sat on the bottom stair trying to listen to what was afoot. My mother appeared to be in pain. I wondered if it was one of her bad headaches. Whenever I asked any questions I was told to get out of the way and go outside and play. I did move outside but stayed close to the door so that I could hear what was going on. There was the sound of clinking cups and saucers coming from the kitchen. I could also hear muffled voices. Then I heard my father saying he must send for Dr. Munro. There were no telephones on or near the farm in those days. My father had to cycle the five miles into Spalding to get the doctor. After what seemed a very long time I was aware of a horse and trap trotting along the cinder road towards our house. Then someone said "Good morning Doctor." My father was with him. It had been very worrying and I wondered if my mother was going to die. By now it was afternoon. I heard the doctor coming down the stairs and then the sound of the horse and trap moving along the cinder road on the return journey. My aunt Emma called me into the house telling me that I could go upstairs and see what the doctor had brought. I ran upstairs as fast as I could. This was indeed the surprise of my life when I heard a baby cry. My mother told me: "Come and see your little brother, here he is in my bed." I just touched his small hand. I was soon bustled downstairs again by my aunt Emma. All the other people had left the house again by now. My aunt Emma was staying to look after us. We were now a family of five.

My mother was unwell for some months after the birth of the baby so my parents decided they would have my cousin Nellie to stay with us for a while to help a little with the housework and look after us. She was twelve years of age and one of a large family. Her father was in the forces serving in France. She spent most of her time looking after us older ones. She shared my bedroom. I thought it most unfair as I had to go to bed early while she would be allowed to stay up until later. She was supposed to be on her holidays I was told. She played games with us and usually won. When we went out walking she often played tricks, like telling me to hurry because there were some gypsies coming for us. I was really afraid of the gypsies when I was very young,

16

often having bad dreams about them. On one or two occasions I awoke after such dreams and my father had to fetch me downstairs for a while until all traces of the dream had vanished. Nellie liked taking us through the fields for walks. There were cows in one grass field which I found very off-putting, when she told me they were looking at me and made us run to get out of their way. I could run as fast as anybody but on windy days I had difficulty because I couldn't hear where they were going and missed them. On calm days it was easy to follow other people because one could hear their footsteps and the lack of sight is no hindrance. But in windy, boisterous conditions it is hopeless trying to follow some-one. Whenever I became lost in a field my first thought was to get to the edge and follow it round to the gate. If there was wire netting round the field it was very easy to trace the way out. Of course there are all sorts of sounds to guide one, such as chickens clucking or trains whistling in the station. Quite a lot can be learned by just standing still and listening. I recall the day when I fancied I heard a cow in a field and so I crept under the barbed wire to get into the next field and tore a piece out of the back of my dress. There was quite a fuss when I got home. I was sent to bed in tears. My mother had mended the tear by next morning. Nellie helped with dressing and undressing the younger children. I could dress myself from being quite small. We wore masses of clothes in those days. First a vest, then a liberty bodice, thick knickers with elastic in the legs as well as the waist, two petticoats, one of them flannel, a dress, and a pinafore.

On the whole we spent some enjoyable times with our cousin although she did get us into some scrapes. She had a great gift of being able to tell us stories all composed as she went along. One day we had a very frightening experience. We were playing in the yard and decided we would see who could climb to the top of a haystack first. We appeared to be doing quite nicely when Nellie called out that she was sinking. I remember I jumped down and hurried to the house and told my mother to come quickly. Immediately my mother ran to Nellie's rescue and managed to pull her out safe and sound, and none the worse for the experience. Then there was the day when I was in trouble. The men were thatch-ing a straw stack in the yard when I ran along the straw to find my father for some reason. I fell and bounced off a heap of straw on to the sharp edge of a pail containing water and cut my forehead deeply. I remember my father carried me into the house and as we went I could hear the blood dripping on to the straw. My mother cleaned up the gash and tied a large handkerchief round my head. I suppose had it been today I would have had a couple of stitches. I was sent to bed out of harm's way for a while.

Here we are in the autumn of 1915. Our baby brother is five months old. My mother is much stronger and nearly her old self again. Nellie's father had come home from the war on leave. Now her mother needed her at home. She returned home in time for Christmas.

Early in 1916 things began happening to me. My parents seemed to be talking about me. I concluded it was concerning me because when I appeared they stopped talking. They were talking about me going to school. There were letters coming to the house. Then one afternoon I knew there must be something afoot. My mother called me into the house and dressed me in my Sunday dress with a clean bow of ribbon in my hair. I was told to sit quietly in the front room. There I found my father with another man who talked to me and told me that I would soon be going to school. My father had approached the local education department in Spalding who sent an officer to interview me.

Once again I was the centre of attention. I found the prospect of going away to school quite exciting. I didn't mind a bit about leaving home at that stage. On the other hand my mother dreaded it. It was my father who was all for it. As the days passed preparations got into full swing. The list of clothes to be taken to the school stated four of everything. My father talked to me about this, and told me that I was going to a blind school in York sometime in May. I forget the date. He also said it would be a long ride in a train. So one Saturday afternoon, while my father stayed at home to look after the rest of the family, my mother took me on the train to Spalding, shopping for material for my clothes. We bought calico for nightdresses, winceyette for petticoats, and material for two dresses, a green one and a navy blue one. She made everything herself, even knitting socks and crocheting the lace edging for the nightdresses and petticoats. This was my first shopping expedition with my mother. She used to say she could be much quicker on her own. The walk to the station along the cinder road took twenty minutes and the train ride about ten minutes. In good weather my father would take us to meet her to carry the shopping.

Unless one could ride a bicycle there was no alterative but to walk since there was no other transport. We did have the use of a horse and trap but on this occasion this wasn't possible, for my father had to look after the other four children. We arrived back home with all our parcels and lots of hard work for my mother. At least she did possess a sewing machine to make her task easier.

During the next few weeks there was never an idle moment for my mother. Her days were pretty fully occupied with the general routine of work. Therefore all the work of making clothes was done during the evenings, often late into the night when everyone else was in bed. From my room I could hear the rattle of her sewing machine which seemed to go on for ages. On reflection she must have worked two days in one.

After the sewing was finished and the garments all ready, everything had to be marked with my name. My father did this by stamping my name on tape which had to be stitched firmly to each garment. Even then some of my clothes got lost at school.

During these last few weeks before going to school, while my mother was bathing and dressing the baby with me sitting in the rocking chair beside her, she taught me several things, the grace which I should say before and after meals, such as "Be present at our table, Lord." Someone had already taught me "Gentle Jesus". From her I also learnt the address of our house. She was always on to us about saying "please" and "thank-you".

Someone made me a present of a purse. Grandad gave me five shillings to put into it. I can remember having it changed into pennies so that it looked a lot. This was quite a lot of money in those days. It was the first time I had any money of my own. My father bought me a dress basket in which to pack my clothes. It had an expanding lid, and could be strapped up neatly after packing. The other girls seemed to have suitcases. I think the basket was lighter in weight. I wonder if that was the idea as my father would be the one to carry it. This basket was lined with waterproof material and lasted for years, surviving all kinds of rough weather.

3.

AWAY TO SCHOOL

This is early May 1916 and the day my brother and I had to leave home to go away to the Kings' Manor School for the Blind in York. Since this is my story I will try to record only my own feelings and experiences. This day was to shape the pattern of my life. The aunts, uncles, and grandparents had been to see me and said their goodbyes with lots of advice to be a good girl. There was much activity in the house from a very early hour, for we were to get the first train to Spalding, because my father was taking us and had to return the same day.

My mother cooked breakfast and packed ham sandwiches to eat on the journey. I wore a green dress with a white collar which my mother had made. There was a pocket in the dress to hold my purse. She had made ringlets in my hair which was tied at the back with a bow of white ribbon. Socks were not allowed so I wore long black stockings as stated in the school clothing list. I remember sitting in my navy nap coat and velour hat much too early. My clothes were packed in the dress basket which my father had strapped up and duly labelled. Norman, the odd job boy, was to take us to Counterdrain station in the horse and trap which we could use.

I remember that the horse, Soldier, a retired war-horse, was a bit tricky at times. He was smaller than the other horses in the stable but my father liked him and knew his little ways. The horse and trap were standing outside the front door waiting to take us. Before Soldier would start on the outward journey a certain ritual must be followed. He had never got out of his army routine. To get him to move my father must stand up in the trap, gun in hand, and fire off one blank cartridge, then drop his gun and Soldier would start off at a trot without more ado. Whereupon my father sat down upon the seat beside us. Norman was in charge on this occasion. There was never any trouble on the return journey, for when he was on the way home he simply made for his stable and food. This was our means of transport for many years while we were away at school. There were some very rough winter nights when returning home for our school holidays at Christmas when Norman or some other person on the farm met us at the station. The cinder-track road to our house after rain or snow was so slushy and wet that one could hear the water splashing over the wheels of the trap. In the war our only means of lighting was a stable lamp partly blacked out hanging on the front of the trap.

As already mentioned the horse and trap were waiting outside the front door. My mother with our last baby brother in her arms, about one year old, was crying when she kissed us goodbye. She stood on the doorstep with the other children. I did learn later that she did not eat any food for a week after we left home because she was so upset at our going. I didn't feel at all sad. I felt quite excited, so much so that I didn't sleep very well that last night at home. It always excited me when things were moving, especially when I was the object of attention. My father lifted us into the trap and after one shot from his gun, sat down beside us. I never gave a thought to my mother and the children standing on the door-step seeing us off.

Off we went down the cinder track road to Counterdrain station. After depositing us and our luggage in the waiting-room, Norman made his way back to resume his normal day's work on the farm. We bought the tickets and boarded the train to Spalding. The train was already standing in the station. This first journey was about ten minutes long. We were soon seated in the York train. I was told it would be a long ride. I knew all about long rides because I remembered my trip to London to see the eye specialist. I think it was my brother's first ride in a train. I was quite excited about it all. He was scared out of his wits in the tunnels. He screamed at the darkness and the noise. My father very soon got him sorted out, and he didn't bother about the later ones.

There were quite a few people in our carriage. I could tell by the rustle of the pages that they all, including my father, were reading newspapers. I recall that it was a warm day and my father had taken off my heavy coat and placed it on the rack. In 1916 the trains were much slower and crowded with servicemen. We reached Lincoln where lots more people came on board, some standing in the corridors. Some new people came into our compartment. I soon made myself known to them. Until then nobody had spoken to me, they had all been too busy reading their newspapers. I remember being given some money which I shared with my brother.

We ate the ham sandwiches packed for us by my mother. My father had bought us a bottle of pop from the refreshment trolley on Lincoln station. We were held up at Lincoln for a long time. I felt very impatient to get to school; I wasn't at all bothered about leaving everyone, at least not yet.

After what seemed to me an eternity we slowly steamed into York station. My father, clutching us and our luggage, helped us along the platform and up several flights of steps out of the station. This huge station with its steam and loud train whistles blowing was really frightening. Once outside the station my father enquired the way to the Yorkshire School for the Blind, Exhibition Square. There were several cabs outside the station. I imagine they were horse-drawn and I think the fare was around two shillings. That was far too expensive for us. Someone helped my father with us to cross the road opposite the station and set us on the right track for the school. I can't remember us having any difficulty in finding our way.

We came to the large gates which led to Exhibition Square. We crossed the square into the school drive and walked down the gravel path to the school entrance. My father pressed the doorbell, where a maid in white cap and apron answered our ring. She invited us into the waiting room which had coconut matting on the floor and told us to sit there and wait. She left us for a long time sitting on a hard seat with no back. I examined the tall cupboards immediately behind us.

After some time the door opened. Someone said: "Hello, I'm Matron." She shook hands with my father. Then she took both my brother and me telling us that we were going to have milk and biscuits. We were taken into what they called the sewing room. This was where all the school's mending of clothes and stockings was done. Meanwhile I assumed my father would be coming to say goodbye to us. Matron handed us over to the sewing mistress. This room was the sewing room but was often called the work room. Our milk and biscuits were put before us while we sat at a long wide table all piled with linen waiting to be repaired.

I put out my hand to feel it. The off-duty maids would help with this sewing during the afternoons. Someone took off my coat and hat. We sat on stools to eat our refreshments. The biscuits were good but I don't remember ever having such things there again. Perhaps they were just for newcomers. After this my brother was taken to the boys' side of the school, while another maid took me through the door opposite to the girls' side. I found myself in a long large room known as the schoolroom. I was handed over to the mistress in charge. She told me that it was too late in the afternoon for me to be taken to my appropriate class and that I was to sit down with the senior girls. They were knitting and sewing. I was to spend the rest of the afternoon in this class. There were four of us to a bench. I was introduced to the girl next to me who was told to look after me. This was Maggie who was very kind and wasn't at all bossy. I took to her straight away. All the time I was expecting my father to come in and bid me good-bye.

However, the teacher brought along to me the foot of an old stocking which I was to unravel to find out how useful I was with my fingers. The majority of these senior girls were advanced knitters and were refooting the school stockings. When the worn foot had been cut off they had to pick up the stitches and carry on knitting on a new heel and foot. This class took place twice a week. The girls weren't allowed to talk during the lesson unless to ask questions about the work. Someone decided I was making a mess of my dress with the black wool I was unravelling. So a pinafore was sent for. I protested at having to put this on. It was put over my head and tied at the back. It was very large for me and I didn't like the smell of it. It wasn't as nice as the ones I wore at home which were starched and ironed. I kept wondering where my father was. He wouldn't leave without saying goodbye – but he did!

The lessons for that afternoon appeared to be over. The teacher came to me and asked how I was getting along. I had finished the unravelling and was just waiting. I dare not say that I had finished for fear I might be given more unravelling to do as the old wool was so matted and not very pleasant to handle. The teacher asked where I had put all the wool I had pulled undone. I said, "Down on the floor." "On the floor!" echoed a very cross voice. She dismissed the class and told me I would have to stay to pick up all the mess of wool from the floor before I could go. I didn't like doing this at all. The floor was very dusty and I was wearing my new dress for the first time. She remained sitting at her desk until I had picked up every little bit of the old wool which I had to put into the wastepaper basket supplied by her. I wondered why I wasn't given one at the outset. I took off the pinafore and laid it on the seat where I had been sitting. She came to take me from the room and, seeing my pinafore on the form, insisted upon my putting it back on again as all the girls under ten must wear pinafores. She then took me into the junior girls' play room. She introduced me to two small girls, Annie and Edith, both of whom were younger than me.

School had finished about four-thirty. There were about eight girls under ten years of age. There were two totally blind teachers who performed after-school duties - Miss Bell, who taught in the school, and Miss Branton, who taught in the technical training section. With hindsight I must say that Miss Bell was a very good teacher albeit rather strict. Those going through her class had to work very hard. She gave us work such as spelling to do out of school. We were given about six words a day to learn as well as mental arithmetic. Work was handed out in the morning class and she wanted to hear the answers at five in the afternoon. During fine weather she walked around the garden with us in turn and heard our answers. We didn't go out in the garden during dark nights. However this first night at school Miss Bell was on duty. It was the task of the two blind teachers to look after the purses and money of all the girls under fourteen. Miss Bell was the person chosen to look after my purse.

Now one piece of advice my mother had drummed into me was that I must not give up my money to anybody. She took hold of my hand to lead me into the garden and asked if I would like to let her have my purse to look after for me as she did the other girls. I would not hear of it as my mother had told me never to let anyone have it. She tried a little persuasion saying I could spend threepence a week on what sweets I liked and also could buy things like toothpaste and scented soap and hair ribbons if needed. So the matter was left for the time being. She put me into the hands of two little girls walking round the garden and asked them to show me the way around.

Whatever the time of year during daylight hours we had to

be out in the garden in the fresh air. So unless it was wet we spent all our spare time out there, even a quarter of an hour before breakfast. During winter we had to wrap up in coats, shawls, hoods, scarves, and anything to keep us warm. Some of us could keep warm running and chasing around. But there were some little ones who didn't move very quickly, probably they were rather timid or slow for some reason. Perhaps they hadn't had the space round their homes as I had on the farm. On the whole most of us were very lively and some of us rather boisterous. We got more tellings off than the quiet ones. My first day at school was during summer weather in May time, with daisies on the back lawn and laburnum in bloom: it fascinated me with its blossom hanging down like chains. The laburnum tree grew just outside the door to the entrance. There was a pathway leading all round the garden.

I understood that eighteen times round the garden was one mile. Some of us used to try to walk one mile before breakfast. There were large lawns in the front and the back of the garden. On the front lawn there was a sundial, flower beds, and a rockery and on the back lawn a huge tree. I believe it was a silver birch. Let us take a walk all round the garden. To the left from the entrance, first the laburnum tree, then the servants' lawn, their quarters, and the boiler house. Then the path turned and, along the left, there were bushes and high railings; to the rear of these were the museum gardens. These gardens are pretty well known and attract lots of visitors, particularly Americans, to view the historic relics especially St Mary's Abbey. This path was a long one, the whole length of the garden. Then turning along the path at the back of the garden, on the left was a high wall with a bowling green behind it. One could tell when a bowling match was in progress because of the smell of the men's tobacco smoke. On the centre of this wall on our side was a rose tree. It was very much loved by our blind teacher, Miss Bell. When the roses were in bloom she very often wore one in her buttonhole. I never knew their colour but they did have a sweet perfume. I learned many years later that when Miss Bell died prematurely no more roses appeared on that rose tree.

Now the last turn. On the left, flower boxes and bushes, then the principal's lawn which contained a crab-apple tree halfway along. If we thought that no one was around we would knock some apples down by shaking the tree. All the time one of the girls with some sight would keep watch to make sure we weren't caught. I managed never to get caught. There was a coincidence when one girl had to go to the sanatorium with a tummy ache. The doctor asked if she had by any chance eaten any crab-apples!

Further along was a path to the left leading out of the grounds. We have gone full circle and come back again to the entrance. There were two summer houses, one of them quite large with a table and seats and ivy climbing over the roof. The girls' quarters were much more attractive than the boys' who had only a large concrete playground with little shade from the sun. Football and cricket matches were played. There was also a skittle alley and a shed with seats. There were toys which had been donated to the school and some girls had their own dolls and prams, toy teasets, etc. I didn't have any toys of my own as my mother had said I was too big for all the old rag dolls.

On Sunday afternoons from three to four we were read to for a few weeks by a lady who had lost her husband and four sons in the war. She gave each girl under ten years old a doll especially made for her with a dress the colour of her choice. The dresses were trimmed with lace and all the clothes could be taken off quite easily. She showed a great interest in all our out-of-school activities and I can remember making her daisy chains.

During the summer months lessons were sometimes taken in the garden. We were called indoors just before six o'clock to wash and tidy ourselves before tea at six. My two escorts, Edith and Annie, showed me into the washroom where there were four wash bowls in a row under the window for washing downstairs. There were about four rows of pegs, each one numbered.

We each had our own peg on which we kept our towel and cotton bag containing brush and comb. This was before the younger ones had a nurse. The school didn't employ a nurse to look after the little ones until three years later, so in those days the senior girls looked after them. As I mentioned, Maggie, who was about seventeen, was asked to keep an eye on me. I got on very well with her probably because she let me help myself. I didn't like people washing my face. I was eight and big enough to do it myself. She treated me gently when combing my tangled hair. We became friends and after she had left the school we kept up a correspondence for a long time.

26

Kings Manor, York.

D. H. Hield.

The Yorkshire Blind School where Hilda Roberts was at school

The author in her late teens

The senior girls over sixteen were in technical training for jobs outside. They learned the usual handicrafts: how to operate the knitting machines, both the round and the flat machines. The latter was the more interesting for garments such as suits, dresses, and jumpers, could be made. When finished off by a skilled person they were quite smart. A few went to college to learn shorthand and typing. The boys attended college to learn piano tuning. Some pupils attended the Royal Academy of Music including Kathleen Torr, one of the girls around my age who also did singing. Many years later, long after our school days, I heard her sing on the North Regional Radio as it was then. At school her piano playing was a pleasure to listen to.

The tea bell rang at six on my first night at school. We were formed into two lines in the junior playroom, the juniors at the front and the seniors bringing up the rear. The sighted teacher on duty that night, Miss Ingleby, walked along with us. I had already taken a dislike to her for it was she who had made me pick all that wool off the floor during the afternoon.

It was about this time that I began to feel worried about the money in my purse should I lose it. It was very well pressed down in my pocket. It was the first money I had ever possessed of my own.

The dining hall was quite huge with tables down both sides. On the right side the first table was for junior girls and the second for senior girls. The boys, juniors and seniors, were on the left side. In the centre of the hall was the serving table. At the far end there was a table for staff but this was only occupied by the master on duty at breakfast. Other meals were taken in the staff dining room. Their food was different from that of the pupils. In the morning the smell of toast and bacon often made our mouths water. As we filed down the passages to our dining hall we often got a whiff of the staff meals. The roast beef, for instance, smelt most appetising, just like that at home. It made us quite envious especially if we had just had a stew with fat meat, that tasted awful, and smelly potatoes. The food during my time wasn't at all good. The cabbage was particularly grim.

At that time there were just over seventy pupils - thirty-two girls and forty-three boys. The noise of chatter in the dining hall was tremendous.

We sat on long forms on either side of the tables. Since this was my first time the mistress on duty placed me on the junior table between two other girls, one of whom was totally blind although the other had some sight; the younger was five years old. Now the two blind teachers who did out-of-school duty in the evenings didn't take any meals in the staff dining room. Miss Branton sat at the head of the junior table. Miss Bell was at the head of the senior table. They did not have meals with the sighted staff but enjoyed the same food. I had to be very hungry to eat the bread and marge dished out to the pupils. I was too upset to eat my first tea so the thick doorsteps scraped with marge didn't bother me. If any was left it would appear again at breakfast the next morning. Breakfast every day was bread and marge, with porridge in addition twice a week. Tea was also bread and marge with jam on Tuesdays and a piece of hard cake on Sundays. Those who didn't like the cake would swop with somebody who did. I happened to like it so, as I had my Sunday sweet ration, I would exchange a couple of dolly mixtures for a piece of someone else's cake.

On the fifth of November the cook made parkin for tea. I liked this and had some of the other girls' as well. The extra cake went down well on Sundays because I usually left my dinner. Matron would often come round and try to make us eat the food. She even tried feeding the little ones who left food, but I don't remember her trying it with me. The food did improve a little I understand after my time there. I believe public schools generally didn't enjoy very good food in wartime. Many years later I read a book called *A Blind Musician Looks Back*, by an ex-pupil of the school, the late Alfred Hollins, who went on to the Royal Academy of Music. He attended the school in the nineteenth century and one chapter is devoted to it. The food then sounds to have been pretty grim. There was no cloth on the bare wooden tables which had a division down the centre. The only luxury they had then was jam on the Principal's birthday. At least we had oilcloth on the junior table even though it was wartime.

Back to my first teatime. At the end of the meal the Principal took prayers. Sometimes they were taken by the master on duty and took the form of a hymn, which we had to learn of course, then a reading from the bible, finishing with prayers. It was the same procedure at breakfast, usually then taken by the master on duty. However, tea over, boys and girls filed out of the dining hall in their different directions.

It was six-thirty and bedtime for those under ten. I protested as I always did at going to bed; I don't think I ever cried so long. I was made to climb the two flights of stairs and ushered into the pink room. This dormitory took about fifteen girls, beds down each side of the room. There was a small space with a locker between each bed. Some of these girls were over ten, and at that age were allowed to go to bed at eight o'clock. Never had I been so miserable. I had completely forgotten about the purse in my pocket. Someone came and took off my dress and told me they were hanging it in the cupboard as I wouldn't need it until going home day. I would be wearing the school uniform in term time.

My bed was in the centre of the row of beds on the right hand side going into the room. I could manage to undress myself but some of the little ones had to be helped. Someone showed me how to fold my underclothes and tie them in my pinafore and place them on top of my locker in case there should be an air raid in the night. Should that happen we would be awakened by the mistress on our floor and told to get down the passages which had quite thick walls. These walls provided the best possible protection. They had stood the test of time since the days of King Charles the First. The old name for the school was "The Ancient Palace of the Stewart Kings".

I don't remember ever having to get up for an air raid, although Hull, which isn't so far away, was badly bombed. I knew I must wrap up my clothes in a bundle every night and place them on the lid of my locker. These lockers were like a fairly tall wooden box. The inside was for all sorts of odds and ends, gym shoes, any toys we might need, our own shoes for going-home day and a staple in the back on which to hang a toothbrush. Our upstairs towel was hung on the rail at the head of the bed. There was no carpet in the space between the beds. This was all so strange to me. The other girls spoke to me telling me their names. I soon got to know them. We were allowed to talk until the eight o'clock girls came to bed. We were then supposed to be quiet and go to sleep although this was nigh impossible with all the din they made with their chatter.

Now there was one thing I didn't like about the girl in the next bed to me. She made the remark that if anyone went into her locker in the night she would bash them. I was the new girl so she must have been hinting at me. Her locker was between our two beds. Mine being on the other side. Her locker was quite safe from me: my mother had drummed into me so often that I must not touch other people's property.

Whether I got any sleep at all that first night I don't remember: I was so homesick and had so much on my mind. I remembered my purse in the pocket of the dress someone had hung up in the cupboard with our going-home clothes. My father hadn't said good-bye. Then the horrid girl in the next bed throwing out hints about people looking in her locker. I remember wondering what she kept in there. However I asked about my purse next morning and they told me that Miss Bell had taken it to look after for me and that I could spend threepence on Saturdays.

While we were getting washed in the bathroom, which was next to our dormitory, I insisted on washing myself but created a fuss because nobody would hold my long hair back while I washed my neck. When the senior, Maggie, came to comb out my hair it was a sorry mess, just about wet through. The mistress on duty at breakfast told me I should have it cut short next time a barber called at the school. I think he called once a month, first to the boys and then to the girls. He came at around 7.30 in the morning: it wasn't long before I had all my hair cut off. I could hear it dropping to the floor, hair ribbons and all. It was Matron's orders that the young ones must have their hair short. Mine was cut short like a boy's with a fringe. After a time when it had grown a little I had it parted down one side as they thought it suited me better. On looking back it was a bad start. My short hair and the school uniform. The dress had been passed down and was big and long. I had black laced boots which were polished every evening by one of the older girls. I had to help clean the little ones' boots when I was fourteen. The polish didn't come out of a tin. It was a stick of blacking which came out of a jar. It was applied with a brush and then polished off with a velvet pad.

The day began with the rising bell at seven. Before seven-thirty we all must be washed, dressed, and ready to go downstairs, all beds made. Then if fine into the garden until the breakfast bell at eight and out of the dining hall by eight-thirty. Should there be any letters for us the mistress on duty would read them. School bell was at nine when we all went to our various classrooms

30

and the seniors to the technical training department. This being my first day I was placed into the appropriate class.

On Saturdays once a month we had fire drill. There were three dormitories and each one had its separate fire drill. I can't remember what happened in the younger girls' dormitory, but I believe that a teacher fastened a belt round the waist of the child and lowered each one down through the window on to the lawn below, where someone took hold of her and released the belt. The girl then walked away. I do remember the fire-drill after I had moved up with the older girls at the age of fourteen. It was most alarming to me and I hated it. If I could manage to be ill I did but it didn't always work. This escape was by means of a chute. Under the bedroom window was a low wide ladder with about five steps which one had to mount to reach the chute. It was a long sack attached to the window and on fire drill days it was let down to the garden below. We were helped into the chute head first and told to fold our arms. If we struggled our arms could be badly grazed on the way down. The headmaster caught us as we reached the bottom and if we had done it properly we landed on our feet. This was even more frightening from the senior dormitory which was one floor higher and so a longer slide down to the ground. After my time the chute method was discontinued and the belt system only was used.

Always on Saturdays we went for a walk before dinner. The afternoon was spent in the garden either with games or, in the summer, reading and lying on the grass or playing in the summer houses. The teacher on duty would write our postcards for us. We had to send a card home once a week. The halfpenny for the stamp was taken out of our own money.

I eventually settled down to school. I had been given dresses which fitted. They were dark green. Coats were the same colour and we had black velour hats in the winter with the school badge on the front. This was a black eagle on a white background, the emblem of William Wilberforce, our patron. In the summer we wore white panama hats with the same badge. We also wore black gloves which fastened with a button. We were measured for a new green dress every year. The previous dress we took for our second best and wore it whenever we went out walking. These walks took place on Tuesday afternoons, Saturday mornings, and Sunday mornings after church. We enjoyed the Tuesday afternoon walks the best when we were taken to Clifton Ings to wander as we wished to gather buttercups or wild roses from the bushes. Some of us would arrive with our arms full of flowers including may blossom. We had them in jam jars all over the window ledges in our playroom.

My first term was coming to an end and everybody was talking about the summer holiday. Some girls were going to the seaside, despite the war, with their parents. I knew very well that I wouldn't be going away. The harvest would be in full swing and my father working all hours. Nevertheless, my holiday would be quite enjoyable spent out there among the wheat sheaves where my sister and brother and I would have our little picnics.

The last day of term was packing-up day. We emptied our lockers and placed our things on our beds for the maids to pack for us. Not a lot got done in school that day. We were weighed and measured in the morning before going home and then again on our return. I lost weight in term time and gained during the holidays. I remember one summer holiday of six weeks gaining twelve pounds. We grew in height too. This last day of term we did everything for the last time. The last dinner for six weeks. The last class for six weeks. One boy was heard to shout as he barged round the playground: "Hurrah, the last bath for six weeks!"

The last teatime was a special one. The school did us proud for the last night. In front of us on our plate were about five cakes – cream cakes and chocolate cakes, tarts, but no bread and marge. If there had been I doubt if anyone would have eaten it.

When we came to the last bedtime it was all excitement and bustle in our dormitory. The blind teacher, Miss Branton, slept in our room and she let us do what we wanted within reason that night. It was the custom for the younger ones to pair up and sleep two in a bed provided we were quiet and didn't disturb the rest. When we played her up sometimes she threatened she wouldn't allow this on packing-up night this year, but she always relented and let us pair up. Since I was the last comer I had no choice but to have someone who might be without a partner. I got a girl with whom I had nothing in common. However the morning came round in the end. Our own going-home clothes had been placed on top of our lockers.

After breakfast the Principal took prayers and he read the

usual prayer for travellers which, I believe, is in the church prayer book.

This was the end of term, going-home day. Some parents who lived fairly near to the school came early to collect their children. There were about six of us who had to travel a long distance. We were given a packet of sandwiches each to eat on the train journey. It was a long morning for us as our train left around one p.m. We had an escort as far as Lincoln, a nurse from 'the welfare' I think. At Lincoln those of us still left were placed in charge of the train guard. He looked after us very well, bringing us sweets and lemonade, and generally making a fuss of us. The door to the compartment was locked, I suppose for our protection. My father met my brother and me at Spalding. We were on the way home at last. End of my first term.

4.

MOSTLY IN YORK

"Good gracious! Whatever happened to your hair?" said my mother as I ran towards her. That was the greeting on arrival home for my first holiday from school. My mother didn't know that I had had my hair cut very short and the sun had bleached it white. She was furious and was going to write to Matron. She always made me wear a linen hat in the sun and I remember she packed one in my luggage to take back with me. She made these small hats and washed and starched them. I did take one back with me but I can't remember ever wearing it. It was good to be home and the first thing I wanted to know was what was for tea.

We were home for six weeks. The harvest was just about starting. The reapers were being got ready and, as was usual, we had the same six Irishmen living in the new granary. We children saw little of them but my mother had to get in food for them. She cooked their potatoes and huge joints of bacon in the copper in the wash house and, as they were Catholics and didn't eat meat on Fridays, it was quite usual to boil twenty eggs for them. I think I must have been showing off a bit after three months' schooling, for I remember one of my aunts saying, "You needn't come here with your airs and graces." They only wanted to know my old self.

By the end of the six weeks' holiday I began to be fed up with farm routine. Everyone was so busy and my mother was preparing meals all the time, the men's meals and then ours. She would sometimes pack us up a picnic tea to take into the field near the house. It had been wheat this year and we sat amongst the tied up stooks which made a lovely shelter from the wind. My mother hadn't got rid of us for as long as she had hoped for, it usually turned out that after all the sandwiches had been eaten we were under

34

her feet again in the house for the next meal. She used to hope that we would stay out a long time to give her a chance to get on with her work.

The holiday over and our luggage packed there was the customary certificate to be signed by a doctor to say that we hadn't been near any infection or been ill. However, since the doctor lived five miles away in Spalding, and getting there was time consuming, my father would sign it in the name of the doctor and got away with it for many years.

The day came for our return to school. How everyone had grown during the six weeks! Immediately after our arrival back at school we were seen by the nurse from the sanatorium who small-tooth combed our hair, put some horrid smelling disinfectant on the backs of our dresses, and let us go. If anyone were to be found with spots they were detained in the sanatorium and seen by the doctor. Much as I had looked forward to the end of the holiday, the first tea time back I felt homesick and never could eat the thick pieces of bread and marge. I suppose I wasn't hungry because of all the food my mother had packed for the journey. It took several days to settle down to the school food but one did settle down eventually.

This was the first Christmas term with lots of things to look forward to. There were the crab apples on the Principal's tree and if one was first into the garden there would be fallen pears from the tree on the back lawn. It was best to let someone with a little sight have a look before eating because of the probability of maggots. Then the play which was put on the week before the Christmas holiday. I don't remember much about the first one.

My first Christmas term finished with some interesting occasions. A few nights before going-home day there was a Christmas tree in the music room. I believe this was the first tree that the school ever had. The toys were stacked around it. The good folk of York had given a donation towards the festivities. All the little ones received several presents. I remember getting a doll, doll's tea set (something I had always wanted), one or two other small things, and a box of chocolate mice. In later years the school governors allocated so much to be spent on each pupil. We could choose what we wanted. I remember a few years later choosing a workbox, and another time a brush and comb in a box. This was

35

always an exciting evening and really put one in a Christmas mood for going-home day. We sang Christmas carols round the tree with the music teacher accompanying us on the grand piano. After the young ones had been taken off to bed there was dancing, when the boys and girls were allowed to mix but, as I deduced later, it was frowned upon to have too many dances with the same boy. I know as I grew older boys would often say: "Can I have the first dance on Christmas tree night?"

Another memory I have of my first Christmas was managing to read uncontracted braille. I can remember reading a Christmas card someone had brailled. During the Christmas holidays I read it to my mother who didn't believe I could read it. All she said was "Get away with you, you know it off by heart." I was able to convince her when, during the month's Christmas holiday, I received a braille letter, uncontracted of course, from one of my friends who had also been learning braille that year.

1917 stands out as an uneventful year except that at the beginning of the term we had 'flu in the school. I can remember there being only four of us left in my class. The sanatorium was full and even the staff were laid up. Needless to say lessons were interrupted so we who were left rather enjoyed ourselves.

During the war the bread was simply horrid. Those who could see said it was nearly black. Whether this was so, I don't know. On one occasion during the summer many pupils were taken with an attack of diarrhoea. I think I didn't suffer this mainly because I hadn't eaten half my dinner. The trouble arose because the vegetables that day were boiled nettles. I just remember some of the young ones being really ill and a teacher had to be sent for. There was quite a crowd for the toilet and since there was only one upstairs many girls had to go to the downstairs one which was quite a long walk. Everyone was talking about it the next morning. I don't think we had cooked nettles again. Vegetables were quite a problem to obtain in the cities at that time.

The Christmas holiday of 1917/18 was a memorable one. I arrived home with spots and had to be bathed twice a day and had to have clean clothes after each bath. My mother had to rub sulphur ointment over the spots. The extra work of bathing, which meant getting in the tin bath on the hearth-rug, and the extra washing and drying of clothes in the winter were problems. However the spots were soon cleared up. Needless to say a letter went to the Matron from my mother. This was the second letter from my mother to the school, the first having been only the previous term when they had cut off my hair.

This Christmas holiday will stick in my mind for the family was down with 'flu. My father and the wagoner were ill and my sister Mabel had pneumonia. The doctor had to be sent for. The roads were too bad for him to come in his horse and trap, so he had to walk across two grass fields. He ordered my sister into hospital. I remember my mother telling him the icy cold weather out of doors would kill Mabel. The doctor said she would die if she stayed in the cold bedroom. So she was rolled in blankets and one of the workmen on the farm carried her across two grass fields to the doctor's horse and trap. It was an anxious time during her stay in hospital but she got better. Just before the end of the Christmas holiday my father, now over his attack of 'flu, collected my five-year-old sister from the hospital. The cinder-track road was thick with snow. He had to carry her most of the way. The road wasn't even fit for horse and trap. It was after we were back at school and every one else was well again that my mother became ill with pleurisy and things were pretty difficult for my father. He enlisted help from an aunt.

There was a lot of illness in the school again this January of 1918. I spent a fortnight in the sanatorium with a sore throat. Then in the spring I developed swollen glands in my neck. In May I was sent into York County Hospital where I was operated on to have a gland removed from my neck. I had a wonderful time in hospital. After I had been there a week I was put out on the balcony. I had to sleep outside and was ordered plenty of fresh air. There were several other children, including one or two babies. We were aroused at five in the morning as breakfast and washing had to be over by eight when the day staff came on. They gave out the toys to us in bed. We used to sing to the doctors and nurses. Everyone was jolly. Nobody told us off. The food was quite good and nobody minded if we left our rice pudding or anything else we didn't like. I was quite sorry when the time came to go back to school.

That summer I spent much time in the sanatorium. During the day I could play in the garden. I enjoyed all this when everyone else was slaving away at lessons. About the end of June the doctor ordered that I must stay outside day and night. The Principal, the Rev. C. F. Hardy, made me a tent on the sanatorium lawn. Quite often his daughter, Betty, then a young girl in her teens, would come into the tent and read to me. In later years I often heard her taking part in radio plays. I spent a few days out of doors but my bed was taken inside about 11.00 p.m. at night. Then the 'Powers-that-be' suggested I go home as it was thought that I would benefit from farm life and the good food. So I travelled home a month before the summer holiday and returned to school at the beginning of the autumn term in September. By this time I was very much better but the swollen glands kept recurring. It was thought they would clear up when I reached the age of fourteen. They did, and I have had no further trouble since. My parents felt the cause of the trouble was the poor quality of the food at school in wartime after the good wholesome food at home on the farm.

I suppose the highlight of 1918 was the end of the war on 11th November. I don't remember a lot about this but we were all assembled in the gym and sang *God of Our Fathers Known of Old* and *Britannia*. The best thing was that we didn't have to fold our clothes in our pinafores each night any more in case of air-raids. Other than that things remained about the same in the day-to-day regime of the school.

In 1919 I became an 'eight o'clocker', which meant I didn't have to go to bed at six-thirty. It wasn't all play. From seven to eight o'clock in the evenings we were read to by the mistress on duty. Some of the books were very boring to me. It wasn't easy to keep track of the stories for there were three mistresses who read different books and one could become confused. At the time I became an eight o'clocker the books were *The Wide, Wide, World, The Mill on the Floss*, and *Cranford*. On Sunday afternoons about that time we were reading *Pilgrim's Progress*. We did sometimes have read to us very good books and could hardly wait for the next part to be read. Also on Sunday afternoons, after the first reading, we read books of our own choice from the braille bookcase. We had to attend church at 10.30 in the morning and 6.30 in the evening. Those over fourteen must also attend early Communion. Of course by this age one had been confirmed. I remember my confirmation day. It was on a cold November night in 1921 by the Bishop of Beverley. There were twelve of us from the school. We had to attend preparation classes for several weeks previously, given by the Principal, who was a clergyman. Our white dresses were passed down from other confirmations. They were very plain with narrow lace trimming round the Peter Pan collar. We wore veils loaned by the convent adjoining the church and our black ribbed stockings. I wore my going home laced shoes not the school boots as some did.

We had to listen to so many lectures from the blind teacher, Miss Bell, whose class I was in at that age. We all took it very seriously and after the church service some of us cried. Miss Bell's serious talks with us made us feel wicked. She drummed into us what a lot we had to live up to as Christians. In her class we started the first lesson in the morning with a prayer and a text. There was a different text for every day of the month, and by the time we were out of her class we got to know them off by heart. I remember that the text for first day of the month was "Pray without ceasing." We had to attend early Communion on the first Sunday in the month. We were given a cup of tea before going out but nothing to eat. Maybe that was why I felt faint sometimes and had to be brought out of church on one or two occasions.

I lost my Grandma when I was about twelve. This was a great blow. The news came in a letter which the teacher on duty read to me. The writing paper and envelope were edged in black. A black patch was stitched on the left sleeve of my coat.

When I was about the age of fourteen the school formed a company of Girl Guides. The boys had already started a Scout branch. We were attached to the Sea Guides in York and it was they who trained us in working for our badges and getting us up to enrolment standards as Guides and then on to second-class Guides. Some girls reached first-class standards later. I managed to obtain about four badges which we wore on the sleeves of our uniform tunics. After my time they went camping during the summer months.

There were a few little treats during the year. There was the Gala to which we were taken by a teacher. We went on the amusements free. Some of them were forbidden to us as being too dangerous. We took some of our pocket money and bought coconuts and sweets from the various stalls. I remember having a ride on the mat. I can't help remembering it because I lost my mat and slid down the slope without it and grazed the skin off my bottom.   Another treat was when we were invited by a Captain Gregg to his field where we had a picnic tea and joined in sports. We had an egg and spoon race. I fell over and lost my egg but got up again and ran with all my might and was there with the winners but was disqualified because I had no egg. It was good fun.

Then there was the annual school outing to Scarborough. We were taken by train in the morning, had dinner at a restaurant, and seemed to be eating all day. We were taken for boat trips by the fishermen and saw them mending their fishing nets. I remember we had to stay together. Of course the sands and the sea were the main attraction.

During the year of 1922 I became a 'nine o'clocker'. In my time, before one was allowed to stay up till nine o'clock, one had to learn the longer prayers. We were trusted to say them unsupervised. Hitherto we all gathered round the top bed kneeling on the bare floor, and had set prayers in which we all joined, one of the blind teachers hearing us repeat them aloud. A few weeks before the age of fourteen we were handed a braille copy of the nine o'clock prayers and, as soon as we could repeat them by heart to Miss Bell, could become a 'nine o'clocker'. This was good in the summer evenings. After tea we were read to for an hour and could then go into the garden if we had no other chores. For instance, those over fourteen were supposed to polish the little ones' boots as well as our own. We could spend our time reading or knitting. Other than knitting black stockings we were taught fancy knitting, such as pretty patterns in baby clothes, bedjackets, etc.

I knitted myself a dress in wide stripes of basket pattern. I was half way through making this when I was taken ill with a mild form of scarlet fever and was whisked into the fever hospital for six weeks. All my belongings had to be stoved including the dress I was knitting but I am glad to say it came to no harm. Though I wasn't very ill I had to go through the routine, which included lying in bed for a month. I was the only girl from the blind school. The rest of the beds in the long ward were occupied by much younger girls from St. Stephen's Orphanage and their nurse. I was too big for toys and I didn't know the songs they used to sing all day. One of the hit songs of the day was *"What will I do when you are far away and I am blue?"* It was a real bore to have to put up with it all through the day including breakfast. The school sent me braille magazines, the school magazine, and *Progress*, all of which had to be destroyed afterwards. I remember learning many poems from them. I had an advantage over the others for I could read braille with my fingers under the bed clothes in the night.

We were allowed to get up and dress for the last two weeks. It made a nice change to be able to walk about or to sit on the balcony attached to the ward. I jumped for joy the day I was discharged. After a strong disinfectant bath I put on my school clothes and was escorted back to school only to find everyone had gone home for the Easter holiday. A bigger blow came when I was told I couldn't go home for a further week. Apparently they were taking extra precautions because of the little ones at home so I had to stay in the sanatorium with the nurse. The domestic staff were all in residence: one could hear some activity but most of the time it was like a ghost town. I was obliged to spend some time in the garden in the morning as I had to have all the fresh air possible. It was so quiet I felt scared. I wished I hadn't been told about Miranda. She was the ghost who was supposed to live in the attic ward of the sanatorium. At this time I happened to be in the middle ward, next to the nurse's room. It was only at night I felt afraid. All fear disappeared with the morning but I was more than pleased when the week was up and I could go home.

I must say I was made a fuss of whilst I was alone in the sanatorium. The food was very good. For breakfast I had a boiled egg in an egg-cup and a banana. The dinners were good too. I always had second helpings of everything. It was always so tasty, so different from the usual school fare. I ate like a horse considering that I was supposed to have been ill. The nurse was very kind too. She took me for walks and also she and her friend took me in a rowing boat on the river Ouse. I was sent home for my fortnight's Easter holiday when the others were on the verge of returning to school for the summer term.

This same year on arriving home for the Christmas holiday I had a very great surprise. I was thrilled and excited. I found there all wrapped up in shawls, lying on the sofa, a baby sister, Lucy. My mother hadn't mentioned this in letters from home. She was about three weeks old. I remember that Christmas finding in my stocking a bottle of lavender perfume as well as the usual orange and nuts.

On arriving back at school in the January term the girls would not believe it when I told them the news of a new sister. I think

41

that that was the year the school entered a singing competition with other schools in York. For several weeks the music lessons were mainly occupied with learning the songs which were set for the competition. However, it turned out that our school won the second prize. I can remember we all received one shilling and sixpence each. I spent all mine on sweets.

This is the autumn term of 1922. At this time of year we started rehearsing the play we were to perform at Christmas. The play chosen this year was *Princess Ju Ju.* It was a musical. The headmistress and the music master put in many hours of their time training us to the standard required. The last week of term was devoted to dress rehearsals. The perfomance took place on the Friday and Saturday nights. We gave it in the music room before a large audience of people from outside the school. I believe it was a great success and was mentioned in the evening papers. Another year we did some Shakespeare. I can remember taking the part of Nick Bottom, the weaver, in *A Midsummer Night's Dream.* Some of us were in the school choir. We gave occasional concerts in the music room in front of an audience. We were a mixed choir. We were taught part songs and madrigals and had some very good soloists. Some of the younger ones played piano duets. These concerts were always well patronised and of a very high standard. When we were older we often had the opportunity to go to the Theatre Royal where we heard some very good plays. We were also taken round Terry's and Rowntree's factories. We always came away with a gift box of chocolates. On certain Sundays we were taken to the Minster for morning service.

The school's prize-giving day took place during the autumn term. The prizes usually went to the boys or girls who had made the greatest progress in the year. Prizes seemed to consist of braille books or braille writing equipment. I have known even a braille watch. The headmistress gave a prize also for good conduct and general tidiness. Now this year, 1922, I was the fortunate girl to win this prize. I chose a grown-up workbox. I had got my lifelong wish. At last I had got a pair of scissors of my own. The workbox contained all that one needed - cotton reels, needles, pincushion, etc. I was able to sew a bit better now as we had sewing classes some afternoons. I don't remember winning any other prizes. I don't know how I managed to win this one for I know I could not have been this particular mistress' favourite - more the opposite.

42

Some of us had favourite teachers though. We used to ask to sit near them in church on Sundays. As only two girls could sit near at one time, one on either side, we would ask a week or more beforehand. There was one mistress whom I thought was most charming. Should it be my luck to sit on one side of her I was terribly thrilled at being able to hold her hand during the sermon. It didn't seem half as long and drawn-out as usual. I must admit I have slept through many a long sermon. We liked it too when there was a procession on some Sunday evenings. The choir boys processed round the church, some carrying banners and singing a hymn, or sometimes it took two hymns to get round the church. The girls who had a little vision would tell us about the good-looking boys. They would try to attract their attention when they passed our pews. It was very fortunate that the mistress on duty always sat at the back of us so must have been oblivious of what was going on. But you never know! I just had to listen to what the girls had to say. They even knew the names of some of the boys. I don't know how they found them out as we were too well guarded to be able to speak to anyone. It was the same thing when, on Sundays, we were out walking in a long line, two by two, and we often met St. Peter's boys' school walking from the opposite direction. Some girls seeing them could smile and my partner would tell me to smile if a boy was smiling at me. All this happened very quickly for the teacher escorting us was always hovering, keeping us in line.

It was very difficult to speak to the boys in school for there was always someone supervising. Obviously some managed to creep through the net for I know some who paired off in later years. I know of one couple whose music lessons ran one after the other who used to exchange letters, in braille of course, by hiding them under the turned back lid of the piano. Perhaps they were able to meet during the holidays. I'm afraid I had the wrong type of parents, for my mother was dead against blind people marrying. Should I receive a braille letter during the holidays she wanted to know all about it. I'm sure I would have managed to get round that one if the need had arisen by telling a white lie. But it didn't arise.

Then on one occasion when I was in the sanatorium with a sore throat I was the only girl who was up and about. In the attic ward was the only boy in the sanatorium. He was up and just about ready to go back among the other boys. I think he was being treated for spots. I was about fifteen and he might have been a year younger. However, since there were just the two of us in the sanatorium, to save work the nurse brought him down to have his dinner with me in my ward. He had some sight and was, I believe, very helpful to those boys who were totals. We had got to the rice pudding when he asked me if I would be his sweetheart. We talked about how we could get braille letters to each other. We came to the conclusion that we could get the boilerman to pass them on. He was friendly with the boilerman and would ask him to do this. We had hardly completed arrangements when nurse came to take him back to his ward. However, I had second thoughts overnight and the next day when he was brought down to have his dinner again with me I told him I didn't want him and not to write any letters to me. He seemed quite cut up and was too upset to eat any dinner. When they brought in his pudding he refused to eat it. I was asked if I would like it and, since it was one of my favourites, I ate it. He must have thought me hard-hearted. I was discharged from the sanatorium the same day so did not have to have my dinner with him again. I never mentioned this to my friends and didn't hear anything more of him. I know once some letters were found and in all of them were the words "Don't let anyone like a teacher get hold of this". Nevertheless this sort of thing went on long after my time. Though it wasn't possible to meet in term time I know of one or two very happy marriages.

1924 proved to be an important year for me. Round about my sixteenth birthday the Principal sent for me. He asked me whether or not I had thought about my future. I remember mentioning I would like to be a teacher. His remark was: "That would take money, and your parents aren't in a position to help." He told me I must be trained to use the knitting machine so that I could work at home. Also as I would be attached to a home workers' scheme by the Institute for the Blind in Nottingham they would buy off me any socks or stockings I couldn't sell myself. I would spend the next three years being trained to use the round knitting machine. My technical training would start after the summer term when I would join the seniors. I hated the idea of this. It was the thing in those days for the majority of girls to be trained for the round or the flat knitting machines. The flat machine was out of the question for me for one needed to work in a workshop where there were the appropriate staff to finish off and make up the garments. The round machine was only for making socks and stockings of all sizes. My parents had been informed of this I discovered while home for the Easter holidays. They wondered how I could make a living in that remote area. Who would buy the goods I'd made? Who would buy the completed articles?

During the six weeks' summer holiday I had a surprise waiting for me. It was more towards the end of the holiday, 29th August to be precise. On the morning of that day things were happening. My aunt arrived as well as the woman who had been to our house once before when my mother was ill. It was then I began to understand. My mother was to have another baby. The other children had been sent to a neighbour across the grass fields. I didn't want to go with them. I wanted to stay at home and read. Really, it was simply that I didn't want to miss anything. The doctor arrived and stayed all morning. Folks were busy in the kitchen making cups of tea and chattering. Eventually I heard the doctor depart and my aunt came and informed me that I had a new sister but not to bother my mother yet because she was resting. Later on someone brought the baby and placed her on my knee. I thought she was lovely of course. When she was taken back upstairs and the others came home I told them the news and how pleased I was that I had been the first one to see the new baby. There was about a fortnight left of the holiday. It wasn't the same with my mother still confined to bed and another person looking after us. My eldest sister who was about eleven had to look after the youngest, Lucy, the two year old. The harvest was in full swing with my father and the wagoner coming in for meals at odd times. The woman looking after us didn't make the food as appetising as my mother. When we were weighed on our return to school I had lost seven pounds in weight. It was I who chose the baby's name. On saying goodbye to my mother when going back to school I told her to call the baby Audrey. We had been reading a book of that name the previous term and I quite liked it. Sad to say her eyes were also affected and later she was sent to the school in York.

When we arrived back for the autumn term I couldn't wait to tell everybody that I had yet another sister. Some of them wouldn't believe me. There were now seven in the family. She was referred to as the 'harvest baby'.

Now my technical training started in earnest. For the first

hour every morning we were taken by the headmaster for what were called continuation classes. We learned about current affairs, held debates, were read to and on one occasion we were asked to give a ten minute talk. Both senior girls and boys attended these classes. The rest of the day we spent in our various technical rooms. The boys on their side worked in the basket or the brush shops. We were taught how to operate knitting machines by a sighted instructress, and how to cane a chair by the blind teacher, Miss Branton. I was not at all interested although I had to resign myself to the fact that I had to earn a living somehow. I put my energies more to outside activities, working for Guide badges, reading, and dabbling in writing poetry. I was fond of knitting by hand. I could knit some quite pretty patterns, either in making baby clothes or dressing dolls. In those days one wasn't as grown up at sixteen as girls are today. I wasn't interested in music and had asked to discontinue piano lessons when I was having trouble with the glands of my neck. I was told it could be suspended for a while. I never heard anything further. I wasn't very good anyway.

At that time, when I was a senior, dancing was a craze among the older girls. Whenever we had the opportunity we would dance around the room while one of the girls played the piano. We had learned only folk dancing in school lessons. I really enjoyed it. When I became a senior we were allowed out on Tuesday afternoons provided we went in pairs, while the younger ones were being taken out for the usual Tuesday afternoon walk. At that age too we could have our own money and so when we were out, if we could afford it, we could go into a cafe for tea and gooey cakes. We could also let our hair grow but it must be cut into a neat bob. I remember one Tuesday afternoon my partner and I called into a hairdresser and he offered to curl our hair for us. We came out feeling really glamorous. Mine was admired by the other girls. A message from one of the maids said how smart my hair looked. This wasn't to last long for the mistress on duty that night whom I didn't much like made me go upstairs after tea to wash my hair and see that all the curls were out before I next put in an appearance. She was against any make-up too. Most of us used vanishing cream, keeping the jar well out of the way so that it wouldn't be seen. However, next morning I appeared in the dining hall with my usual straight hair. It had been curled with curling tongs which had scorched the hair. A handful fell out but it soon grew again.

In 1925 I became head girl. This didn't involve a lot. If a new tin of boot polish or a fresh tablet of soap in the downstairs washroom was required it was the head girl's job to go and ask for it from the store room.

In 1926 there was a railway strike just as we were about to go home for our Easter holiday. Those who lived close to the school could go but we who lived any distance away and had a train journey just could not get home. It was boring. There were no school lessons. Some of the teachers had managed to get away. There were all sorts of rumours that some trains were running. Twice we were taken to the station and put on a train where we waited ages only to be turned off and told it would not be running. Back we went to school, the Principal meanwhile having sent a telegram to my parents to say I was on my way home. Then another to say I wasn't. We were messed about like this more than once. However we did eventually manage to get away. Once again a telegram was sent to my parents to say we were on the way. We managed it this time, ten days late but we still had the fortnight's holiday.

1926 was to be my last full year at school. I didn't look forward to leaving. I always had it in the back of my mind that I was worth something better than just knitting socks all day. Just before the end of the Christmas term I was once more sent for by the Principal. He gave me a box all tied up with paper and string. The governors of the school presented it to me with their good wishes for the future. It was a set of chair caning tools, hammer, punches, clippers, knife etc. He also told me that they had bought me a knitting machine which would be dispatched to my home. There was a metal plate attached to the table to which the machine would have to be screwed which said "The property of the Yorkshire School for the Blind".

By the time I had finished with the machine the school had been closed and York University had taken over the premises for administration purposes.

However, on the morning of going-home day, in the prayers after breakfast, we sang the hymn *Lord, Dismiss Us With Thy Blessing*. The tears filled my eyes when we sang the last verse.

"May Thy Father's hand be shielding | Year by year a richer store.
Those who here shall meet no more. | Those returning, those returning,
May their seed time past be yielding | Make more faithful than before."

5.

Boston - The First Time

My school days were over. I was once again back on the farm and I learned from my parents that I would be going to a blind home to see how I got on with my knitting machine. If it turned out that I wasn't happy there I could come home to live and I could also come home for breaks whenever I wanted. Although I hated the job I was about to embark upon I knew I must resign myself to it for the time being. The report from the teacher of the knitting machine department said I would need constant supervision for a while. A new home and hostel for blind women and girls had recently been opened in Boston. It seems that it had all been arranged before I left school that I should go into this home with my knitting machine and become a home worker.

My Christmas present for this year was a new brown coat and hat to match. The coat was trimmed with fur at the neck: the hat had a turned-up brim at the front. I had never felt so good in my clothes. This was the beginning of my interest in clothes, and how I looked, which has never left me. The school had sent me home in my second-best school green uniform. They had given me two dresses both of which were green which I had to wear for a time as my parents couldn't afford to buy me another. I hoped I would soon earn sufficient money to buy one for myself. So my second-best school dress was my best dress and my old everyday school dress had to be my working dress for a while. My mother had bought me two working overalls with long sleeves. I look back in horror when I remember the underclothes they gave me - two striped petticoats, two pairs of combinations, and two liberty bodices! I had my old green school coat for every day and did not possess a mackintosh or dressing gown. I retained my old school boots for every day and had a pair of shoes for best which my mother had bought me the previous summer. I was not allowed to take these back with me to school that last term. The reason was that some years previously I had exchanged a good pair of shoes with an older girl for a piece of hair ribbon. It was a long time before I got another pair of shoes. It was school boots all the time!

Here we were in January and once more my bags were packed as I set off for the next phase of my life. It was a mild Tuesday morning when I arrived in Boston, Lincolnshire. I held my father's arm as we wended our way out of the station. I wasn't as excited as I had been on the day I went to school but was rather apprehensive. Although I call myself an optimist the future looked rather gloomy to me. To begin with I wondered what the people would be like in my new surroundings although I had been told that I would be meeting some younger people. My father enquired the way to the local Blind Home and on the instructions given we found no difficulty. We turned into Pen Street and very soon my father saw the double-fronted house at No. 25 which was our destination. He lifted the heavy door knocker and knocked. I don't remember there being a door-bell.

It seemed a long time before we were admitted. The maid answering the door invited us to go inside and sit down. We were ushered into a fairly large room which was the lounge and dining-room in those days. I sat near a table with a plush tablecloth and tassels. This was removed and replaced by a linen cloth for meals. A feeling of homesickness came over me just as it had done on the first day back at school at the beginning of a new term although this was somehow different. After a few minutes Miss Spencer, the matron, came into the room and introduced herself to my father. Nobody ever addressed me when my parents were with me. My father handed over my luggage to her and, after kissing me goodbye, left for the return journey home.

Many thoughts passed through my head. It was two or three months from my nineteenth birthday. Matron took me round the room and introduced me to the residents. Their ages ranged from twenty-three to seventy-plus years. There were eight residents including myself. The oldest of all was Miss Rose, a very outstanding lady. She stole my heart right away. She was a very refined and erudite person and made much of me. When I felt fed up and bored she liked me to sit on a footstool at her knee and read poetry to her. Then Matron took me upstairs to show me my bedroom. The stairs were the most luxurious I'd ever trodden on. They were thickly carpeted with brass stair rods and highly polished handrail.

Matron showed me into the bedroom which I was to share with two others; Mary was thirty-three years of age and Hilda twenty-three. The three beds were arranged one on either side of the window and the third behind the door. By the side of each bed was a rug and a set of drawers: the small drawer at the top of the chest could be locked if desired. There was lino on the floor. I don't remember there being a chair by the bed. We used to have to sit on the bed. The small chest of drawers was quite adequate for the underclothing I possessed. I was next shown my wardrobe space. This was a row of pegs along the wall of a recess concealed by a thin cotton curtain. I had to share this space with one of my room mates. I didn't possess any coat hangers. I had only one dress to hang up - the other I would be wearing - along with my new brown coat and my everyday old school green coat. There was also a shelf above the hanging space on which I kept my one and only hat. Just across the landing was the workroom where three of us worked on the knitting machines. There was lino on the floor and a radiator heated from the boiler down in the kitchen.

My knitting machine arrived the following day and was set up under the window. There was a large table in the centre of the room on either side of which the other two machines were fastened.

Mr. A. K. Turner, the person responsible for running the home, was a very caring man and pioneered blind welfare in this area. He had the welfare of all of us at heart. He was always willing to listen to our troubles. Should there be any complaints he could always be depended upon to put things right.

I'd learned the way around and unpacked my few clothes when the gong sounded for lunch. There was just the one room downstairs for the residents which served as both lounge and dining-room. The dining table could be extended to accommodate up to ten people, four on either side and one at each end. There were never more than eight of us. Either Matron or a maid was in attendance. After breakfast Matron would conduct a short service, a prayer and a reading from the bible, or perhaps from another book. I found all this rather boring and for those of us who were home workers there were no hard and fast rules as to what time we started or finished work so long as we put in the necessary hours.

The food was excellent most of the time. We usually had cooked breakfast except on Sundays when we had boiled ham. There was also plenty of bread and butter and marmalade but no toast. I never tasted toast the whole of the two years I was in the home. We only got the nice smell of toast from Matron's room at her teatime. The dinners were very good, roast beef and York-shire pudding twice a week, fish on Fridays. We didn't have the terrible stews we had had at school. After the school food, meals at the Blind Home seemed like a banquet. There were often second helpings for those who wanted them. Teas were also interesting, something different every night, if only sandwiches, sometimes with cakes and pastries. Tea at five was the last meal of the day, except for a hot drink and biscuits at nine o'clock. In the evenings we often felt hungry. There was a fish and chip shop a few doors away and the smell sparked off an appetite. I used sometimes to buy a penny packet of chips and smuggle them up to the workroom to share with the other two workers.

Even if we were not working we younger ones used the work-room while the older ones were in the lounge listening to the wireless. They all had headphones. About five pairs were plugged into a socket on either side of the fireplace. The wireless set stood on a high shelf somewhere at the back of the room. There were no loudspeakers in those days. The set ran on dry batteries and a container of liquid called an accumulator which was changed quite often. I rarely listened except for the Saturday-night play. I spent my evenings working on my knitting machine for I was very slow at first. In fact I had some very frustrating days. I just couldn't get on. The ribber attachment dropped stitches if the tension was not just right. It isn't possible to keep the same tension having got it right because some customers wanted three-ply wool, some four ply and, worst of all, some two-ply. A smaller cylinder had to be used for children's hose, and for ladies' two ply wool stockings a fine cylinder and machine needles. The other two girls had a heavier make of machine and seemed not to drop so many stitches. Of course they had been working for some time and were more experienced than I was.

We were encouraged to get out in the fresh air during the day, particularly in winter, and do some work during the evenings. All finished work had to be pressed. The iron we used for the

51

pressing was heated in the kitchen furnace. It is surprising how long it would stay hot. In those days it was certainly all work and not very much play. One evening a week I attended Girl Guides. On Thursday evenings I went to the Girls' Friendly Society meetings. I made friends through joining these organisations. On Sunday evenings a friend, Sister Burton, came to take me to the evening service at Boston Stump. She often took me home with her for supper afterwards. As she lived some way off we had quite a rush as I had to be in by 9.30 p.m.

There were the occasional social evenings arranged by the Blind Society. One Monday every month a musical evening was arranged for us. There was a good variety of entertainment, all by local talent. The programmes were very varied and of a very high standard. On some Friday afternoons we had a reading meeting in the Station Street Institute. Someone read to us for an hour and we had cups of tea and biscuits afterwards. There was a New Year party for the blind in January with entertainment laid on. I enjoyed one or two social outings with the Guides. On one happy occasion we attended a Guide Rally in Lincoln, where I was introduced to Princess Mary. She was interested in my bandaging which was required for my First Aid badge.

My parents visited me quite often and after working for a couple of months I had managed to save one pound. I remember how amused they were when I said I wanted to buy a new dress. I had no idea of the cost. However, we did go into town to look for a new dress. We managed to find one, albeit much subsidised by my parents. I remember it well. It was a pretty mauve colour. What a relief to get away from the school green for best! I felt good in it. Money took a lot of saving then as our earnings were so low. We received eight shillings a week augmentation from the Home Workers' Scheme. To qualify for this we had to earn eight shillings a week ourselves. We were required to pay board to the Home at the rate of ten shillings a week. The actual cost of board was fifteen shillings a week but the balance of five shillings was paid by the Board of Guardians. When I had paid my ten shillings board I had about six shillings left for myself. Of course I didn't always end up with six shillings, for shoes might need mending, or maybe I needed a tube of toothpaste. With all such contingencies pocket money seemed to dwindle away. Every penny mattered. I used to put the money I saved into my top drawer and would watch it grow every week.

After the dress, I was saving for material for making under-clothes. I remember buying six yards of a material called sparva. While I was at home for the Easter holidays my mother made up the material into underclothes for me. The garments were trimmed with lace and replaced the not–so–nice ones given me from school. There was always something to save for. I loved nice clothes and my mother often bought a remnant from the market to make our dresses. She has made me many a dress costing less than two shill-ings. I spent nothing on my hair. 'Perms' were just about taking on and were a luxury.

As time passed I made friends and got out more. With one family in particular, the Brammers in Tower Street, I had my second home. I was welcome any time. I went mostly on Sundays for tea and quite often for the day. They were quite a large family and I spent many enjoyable days with them. To this day Grace is still a very close friend. I didn't like the rule of having to be back at the home by nine–thirty p.m. In those days the railway ran evening trips to Skegness for a shilling. This wasn't possible for me as the train didn't return till ten p.m. Still we enjoyed many picnics and trips down to Freiston Shore.

After I had reached the age of twenty I began to be more and more dissatisfied with my lot. I felt I wanted to be free like other girls. I knew there wouldn't be any more freedom in my own home but I also felt I could not get anywhere living in a home for the blind. My younger sister had a boyfriend. I envied her although she had to comply with rules such as being home by certain times. There was the feeling at the back of my mind that I could do better, especially when people remarked to me that at my age I ought not to be living in a home. The discontent wouldn't leave me. I hated my dull job although I knew very well it was the only way for me. There was no one to whom I could talk about the situation. I kept busy with my work and let the matter rest awhile always hoping something better some day would turn up for me.

About that time I found another friend who escorted me to church on Sunday mornings. I wasn't enthusiastic about church just then but I was glad to get out. My religious leanings were not so strong as they had been at the time of my confirmation, but there was something somewhere that convinced me that there is a divine being worth following on whom I pinned my hopes of doing something more worthwhile with my life.

I remember going to Boston Fair during my stay at the Blind Home. It was the first time I had visited a fair since I left school. My friend and I thought we would like a ride on the cakewalk. As soon as it started to move I knew that I should not have gone on it. My friend had told me what to do and it all sounded very easy but my feet just couldn't get the rhythm of it so that I could do nothing but clutch on to the railings. People kept on telling me to move but I dare not budge. In the end it was switched off for me to get off. It caused a big laugh but I was petrified.

We could hear the fairground organs from our bedrooms. The last tune they played before closing down for the night was *God be with you till we meet again.*

I was fortunate in having so many friends and was often invited out to tea or for walks. However, we were not allowed to invite our friends for a meal in return.

There was one very interesting occasion when friends took me to London for the day so that I could enter for the braille-reading competition held at the National Library for the Blind in Tufton Street. We went by a morning train which in those days went straight through to King's Cross. The readings took place during the morning. Lunch was served in the Library restaurant and the finals were held in the afternoon in Church House, Westminster. It was an afternoon I have never forgotten. The winners read really superbly. I particularly enjoyed listening to the little children. The standard was very high. There were some very distinguished people on the panel of examiners, including Lady Buckmaster and Walter de la Mare who spoke to us. Tea was served afterwards in the National Library but we couldn't stay as we had to get back to Boston.

My nineteenth and twentieth birthdays were spent at the Blind Home. I hoped I might be living at home before my twenty-first birthday. Getting away was always at the back of my mind. The bits of chatter between the matron and residents made me all the more determined. I heard Miss Cable, the new matron, say one day that my parents couldn't want me at home or they wouldn't have allowed me to be in a home. I knew they did as they told me I could go back home whenever I wanted to. I was the only resident with a home and parents. One resident did have a father who was elderly. I spent many hours in the workroom especially in the evenings when I didn't go out.

I also spent many interesting hours with Miss Rose, the seventy-year-old lady, in her corner of the lounge. I sat on a footstool at her knee while she would entertain me with stories of her youth. She was a retired school teacher and had taught in country schools. She was totally blind and did not know braille. There were no talking books then and so for all news and information she had to depend on the wireless or someone reading from the newspapers to her. She spent most of her evenings listening through her earphones. She liked the talks and the Promenade concerts. My taste for good music at that time was rather narrow. It is something that develops over the years. I had a second-hand gramophone which gave me much pleasure though I believe it did annoy some people. I remember the small sixpenny records of the latest hits. I used to drive everyone mad with *Happy days and lonely nights*. One of my workroom friends and I used to burst into song sometimes as we worked. She was rather deaf and a bit off beat so I don't know how it sounded to others. In later years she lost her sense of hearing completely in addition to blindness.

During my time at the home I met a rather remarkable lady, Faith Booth. She was a home teacher of the blind and was herself totally blind. She was responsible for the welfare of the blind in the Holland and Boston area. As she visited the blind in their own homes she often had to travel quite long distances by bus, train, or on foot. It was her job to teach newly-blind people to read braille or, in the case of very elderly people whose fingers were too hard with rough work, the moon system. Some of the moon characters are almost like ordinary print. She took me for a walk once a week. I learned quite a lot from her. I was very naive when I left school. Those two years spent in the home have stood me in good stead through the years. I suppose I had grown up. I had made many friends whom I wouldn't have met had I returned to my home in the wilds after leaving school. I had also developed great patience in sticking to my work, boring as it was. In other words I had learned to stand on my own feet. All the time I was thinking ahead and of how I was going to get away from my boring job.

Whilst I was at home for Christmas, before my twenty-first

birthday, I mentioned to my parents that I would like to leave the Blind Home. They were quite willing for me to go home to live and I could work on my knitting machine in a corner of the front room. I had weighed the matter up and knew very well that I would not get out so much. There were the Guide meetings but I had begun to feel rather old for that and anyway I was nearly twice as old as some of the girls in the group. However my mind was made up. On my return to Boston I intended to tell the powers-that-be that I would be going home to live.

Over Christmas the present for my twenty-first birthday in April had been under discussion. I could have either a gold chain or a new coat and dress. I chose the latter for I loved new clothes and never wished for jewelry.

The next time Mr. Turner, the secretary of the local blind society, visited us in our workroom I mentioned to him that I wished to return home to live. He appeared to understand and his remark was simply: "I hope you will be happy, but if you don't like being at home you will be welcome back here." I hoped that wouldn't happen. If it did it would mean that I had failed. The thought of failure bothered me a lot. It has always bothered me. At about this time a few changes were taking place at the home. Another matron had left and there had been a series of relief matrons. The home was being extended. The whole of the double-fronted building had been purchased by the blind welfare and the residents now had a dining room as well as a lounge. More bedrooms were added and more office space provided.

Preparations for my move went ahead. My knitting machine was dismantled and erected in my own home. I kept wondering if I was doing the right thing. I knew I would keep my friends for I had invitations to visit them whenever I could. This I did and our friendships are still alive today. Taking everything into account my beginning my working life in a home must have paid off for I have never looked back with regret. It is good to get away from the present and look forward to the future. There have been times when I have wished time could stand still, but that was a decade or so later.

6.

HOME FOR A WHILE

My removal home had been completed and the knitting machine had been screwed down to the floor in the chimney corner. The leather easy chair which had hitherto occupied this corner had been moved further back but was replaced again at weekends, or whenever I wasn't working, to hide the machine. The biggest problem was winding my wool. There wasn't enough space in the front room for the wool winder to be fully spread out. All my wool winding had to be done out of doors on fine days. My father had fixed a table outside. There was a wooden partition behind the table which shaded off the cold winds. On one end of the table there was a fixture for the bobbins on to which the wool had to be wound. At the opposite end was my wool winder or 'swift' as it was called. One could get eight ounces of wool on at one time. The swift could spread out to fit any size skein of wool. The bobbins varied in size. Some could take one pound of wool if wound evenly. When the weather was good in winter or summer I would fill up all the bobbins to keep me going for a while. If, as did happen sometimes, there should be a long spell of wet weather and I could not wind out of doors, I had to perform the task in the kitchen. This meant that my mother couldn't get on with her cooking, etc. However, I had to take every opportunity when the weather was good. I have often wound wool when snow lay thick on the ground. I never felt any the worse for it. I was well wrapped up in thick coats and scarves. Fingers became rather cold in freezing weather but warmed up eventually.

Nevertheless this was to be the practice for the next twenty years. I can remember some very cold days and some very hot days. I could get over the problem of the hot days by getting up very early in the morning before the sun came over the table on which I was working. I tried to get through all the machine work by tea time. Each sock or stocking had to be finished off by hand which I could do during the evening sitting round the fire or, in summer, under the elderberry bushes. My father didn't like to see me working in the evenings on the knitting machine.

It was about this time that we had our first radio or wireless as it was called in those days. My brother made it. I liked to sit up late finishing off my work and listening to the late night dance music with the old-type dance bands. If my parents had gone to bed I would often sneak a little more coal on the fire otherwise the room soon became cold.

On 9th April I celebrated my twenty-first birthday at home with my parents and family. I received the promised birthday present of a navy coat and hat with fawn trimming and a pale blue silk dress. I felt good in them and looked forward to wearing them. My Boston friends sometimes invited me to visit them, and would bring me home again and sometimes stay with us. It suited me down to the ground when my friends stayed with us for it meant that I could get out and about a bit more. Grace Brammer would spend her week's holiday with us and at that time one could purchase a railway ticket for ten shillings and use it to travel anywhere in the area every day for a week. We did this a few times. In order to get back home in reasonable time in the evening we were fairly limited on how far we could travel. We did spend some happy days at Mablethorpe and Sutton-on-Sea. One year she took me to stay with her aunt and uncle at Altringham where I was taken to Manchester Belle Vue zoo and other places of interest. She also took me to her other relatives in Northampton. This started a further friendship and they invited me again.

My sisters and I often went out walking. I remember one afternoon we walked into Spalding to the pictures. This was where I saw (or heard!) my first film, *Broadway Melody*. I enjoyed it very much having already learned several of the tunes through listening to the late-night dance bands.

A few years later my two sisters found boy friends and that put an end to our walks together. How I envied them on Saturday and Sunday afternoons when they went out all dressed up in the sunshine! Still, I did break the monotony by visiting friends whenever I could.

The years rolled by; my two sisters married and went their

various ways. My work kept me busy all day and late into the evening. I had become quite fast at turning out the work and could knit a pair of socks in an hour, leaving the finishing off until the evening. The stockings with their shaping took longer. Boys' socks with turned-down tops in the school colours took even longer. I also knitted gents' golf hose with a diamond pattern in the turned-down tops. I got as much work as I could manage, both private and through the Home Workers' Scheme.

In the spring of 1937 I spent a fortnight's holiday with my friends in Northampton. One afternoon during my visit they took me to see round the Institution for the Blind in Gray Street. I was introduced to some of the workers. It was all most interesting. Before we left the secretary called us into his office and talked to us about my job of work. He was quite impressed and suggested that I might like to become a teacher of the blind, that is teaching newly-blind people reading, writing, and handicrafts in their own homes. He told me that some local authorities employed blind home teachers and often helped with the expense of a sighted guide. The idea pleased me. The fact that I had never been out on my own didn't occur to me just then. However, he allowed me to go on visits to a few blind persons in Northampton with their home teacher, a partially-blind lady. This gave me an insight into their work. I also learned from her that it needed quite a lot of studying for the examination. This lady, Enid Murray, was a real help. She advised me as to what books to read on blind welfare and also where to obtain all the relevant material on matters such as pension schemes, education acts, insurance, employment and so on.

When I told my father what I had in mind to do in the future if I could obtain the necessary qualifications, his remark was: "Anything's better than the knitting machine." It gave me a different outlook on life in general. With the exception of one book, *The Home Teacher's Handbook*, all the relevant material was printed matter and all of which had to be read to me. All my notes I had to make in braille. My studying had to be done after I had finished the day's knitting. My young sister, Lucy, aged ten years, was always willing to read to me the GPO leaflets about pension acts, insurance, employment, etc. She must have found it very boring but she never complained. I had to depend a great deal on my memory. Then the vicar of our parish, the Rev. H. H. Stainsby, read some of the printed material to me on an occasional visit.

The winter of that year was a very busy one for me. I learned to read in the moon system. This method of reading is usually taught to people losing their sight in later life. One cannot write in moon as one can with braille. The syllabus for the home teacher's examination contained seven subjects: braille, moon, professional knowledge practical, professional knowledge theoretical, and three handicrafts. I added a fourth handicraft in case I failed in any of the others. My crafts were hand knitting, chair caning, raffia baskets, and rugmaking. I was quite familiar with all four having learned them at school and had obtained my basket badge while in the Guides. The only two subjects I had to learn from scratch were how to read moon and the deaf manual alphabet for communicating with the deaf/blind. I remember it to this day. During the winter of 1937 I took no breaks at all from work, in fact I often spent hours in bed under the bedclothes reading moon books. I needed a great deal of practice to gain some sort of speed. The only way was serious reading.

In March of the following year I sent in my application form to sit for the examination of the College of Teachers of the Blind. I was accepted to sit the examination in early May. It took place at Swiss Cottage Blind School in London. Since my parents would never hear of my going to London alone Daisy Hovey, the home teacher in my area at that time, went along with me as my guide. She escorted me to the accommodation which had already been arranged for me where the lady in charge took me under her wing and was most kind and generous.

I had to stay in London three days for the examination. As I knew nobody she took me for walks in the evening. The first night we went to see the film *Escape Me Never*. My mind wasn't in the right state for me to enjoy it for I was worrying about the next day's examination. I must not fail as this might be my one and only opportunity of getting away from my dull old job. The three days soon passed and someone from the school saw me on to the train back home. My father met me at Spalding where I had to change for Counterdrain. I had found that the written paper "theoretical knowledge" was very long and difficult, especially for someone with no experience in the work, but the others had not been too bad.

Six weeks elapsed before I received the letter with the results of the examination. I could hardly contain myself while the letter was being opened. I had failed in the written paper "professional knowledge theoretical" but I had passed in the practical side and all the other subjects. I had got honours in braille and chair caning. It was disappointing failing the written paper which I had been allowed to do in braille. I was very upset at the time. However, I could take this one subject again the following year. So I had to spend another winter reading all the books and leaflets on blind welfare I could find. I dug into the history of blind welfare right from the days of Queen Elizabeth I.

The following May, 1939, I again went to the Swiss Cottage Blind School for one morning to take the subject I had failed the previous year. I remember feeling rather nervous and unsure of myself. I answered all the twelve questions this time. In view of all the reading I had done I was able to elaborate more on some of the items.

I remember the spring and summer of 1939 were particularly beautiful. It was about the middle of July when I received the results of the examination. This time I had passed. I had been successful in obtaining the Certificate of the College of Teachers of the Blind (the home teacher's certificate). I felt on top of the world. Now I could try to secure a post somewhere.

We were now in August and there was talk of an impending war with Germany. I joined my Boston friends for a holiday in a caravan at Ingoldmells, near Skegness. It was one of the happiest holidays I have ever had. There was a veranda to the caravan. After our swim in the sea in the mornings we would lie in our bathing costumes and sunbathe on the veranda. The weather was glorious and we even had a moonlight picnic down at Gibraltar Point. We didn't give a thought to the impending war. We did not realise how near to war we really were.

Wherever one went there seemed to be nothing else to talk about but war. My father thought we must have a reliable radio to get the daily news so the old home-made set with the headphones was put away and a new four-valve set with a separate loudspeaker was bought. The loudspeaker was like the old-fashioned gramophone horn and could be moved from the front room into the kitchen if required. We still had the batteries and the accumulator to bother with. My mother was hoarding all sorts of goods she reckoned we might not be able to buy when war came. I remember all the tins of salmon and bags of sugar stacked away, not to be used until the war came. Even the Irishmen working on the farm for the harvest were panicking in case they couldn't get back to Ireland. In fact some of them did leave for home well before war was declared. My mother bought yards of blackout material and spent the evenings running up curtains.

I had spent the week prior to the outbreak of war with my friends in Boston. I decided to return home on Saturday. While I was waiting at Spalding station for my train to Counterdrain several trains arrived with hundreds of evacuees, largely from the King's Cross area of London. There were very many children and women carrying babies. I understand they were a very pathetic crowd. Hundreds of them disembarked at Spalding and were taken off in coaches to be billeted in private houses of families in the area. The station sounded like a noisy fairground with all the chatter and the screaming of children. I was by now quite convinced that there would be a war. It saddened one to think of all these people having to leave the comfort of their own homes to be placed in such strange surroundings. I spoke to one evacuee who had been placed with our station master and his wife. She was carrying a very small baby. Her husband was already in the Army. I learned later that this woman soon returned to London because she was too lonely living in the country. She came from a very vulnerable district where the bombing was pretty bad later on. I often wondered whether or not she survived.

The 3rd September, 1939, was a sunny Sunday morning. We all gathered in our front room. My father invited the Irishmen to come in and hear the announcement by Mr. Chamberlain on the BBC. After the stroke of eleven his voice came through loud and clear. We were at war with Germany. After what seemed to me a long silence the Irishmen left the house to return to their quarters. I took all this very seriously. My father thought it would all be over by Christmas. I thought how could anyone tell how long it would last. We knew that Germany had been preparing for war for some time. We didn't appear to be anything like prepared. One listened to the news from foreign stations in English but it was difficult to form a balanced view of the situation. There were so many conflicting reports. In the event of an air raid we couldn't hear the siren, living as we did so far from the town.

However, things carried on much as usual. We wouldn't have known there was a war on at first. I continued to receive plenty of orders for my knitting. The Home Workers' Scheme allowed me a wool ration of twelve pounds per month. I could also purchase extra wool from the Spalding shops. I had started doing hand knitting. There seemed to be a big demand for baby clothes. I made little coats and dresses, bootees, and mittens. There was very little reward for hand knitting but it made a welcome change from the machine.

I don't remember when rationing really started but we knew no shortage at Christmas. When clothing coupons were introduced it affected my orders for work. The requirement was two coupons for a pair of socks and three coupons for a pair of stockings. A coupon-free wool-and-cotton mixture could often be obtained from the market. This was quite satisfactory for baby clothes. It was rather fine and went a long way so it was quite successful financially.

Meanwhile, I answered one or two advertisements for home teachers, only to be told that a fully-sighted person was wanted for the post. Some local authorities who normally employed a blind person were evacuating them to a safe area. After a few unsuccessful applications I decided to abandon the idea until the war was over, little thinking it would go on for nearly six years.

In the 1939 war one of our greatest assets was the radio. I seldom missed a news bulletin. I enjoyed the plays and variety programmes with all the well-loved themes and players - Rob Wilton, Gilly Potter, Norman Long, Elsie and Doris Waters, to name but a few. Then there were the talks on Sunday evenings by J. B. Priestley. How I remember his words: "Two tins of Spam in the cupboard and a new overcoat don't spell security." Then I remember songs which helped keep up our morale: *There'll Come Another Day* and *It's a Lovely Day Tomorrow* and so on. For me, who didn't get out very much, it lessened the boredom.

In February 1940 there came the biggest shock of my life up to then. My father contracted 'flu which turned to pneumonia. He died in Spalding Hospital after a few hours. He was just about to become a pensioner and was looking forward to his retirement. My parents had already been included on a housing list for a new house a few miles away.

The winter of 1940 was one of the sharpest I had experienced.

Our roads were frozen hard and snow piled up over the fields. The cold was so intense that I felt I would never be warm again. After about six weeks my mother was offered a small cottage at Spalding Common. She accepted as a last resort for it was terribly lonely on the farm, particularly when the workmen had left for the night. Sundays were worst as there was so little activity except for the man who put in a brief appearance to feed the animals.

After nearly twenty-seven years we were on the move again and we were installed in a small cottage at Spalding Common. There were eight of these cottages in a row. We had brought our dog, Nigger. Some years previously he had replaced Mick who had lived for sixteen years and it had been a sad day when he had had to go. Although the cottage wasn't quite large enough for our requirements, it looked very cosy and bright, I understand. The garden was much too big for my mother to manage. After the quiet of the previous house it was very noisy, particularly at night. There was the railway at the back of us with goods trains carrying materials for the war effort all night and, on the main road at the front of the cottage, heavy lorries carrying further goods for the war effort passed at all hours. Then there were our bombers passing over to raid Germany just after dusk as well as the German bombers coming in. I could tell which were the German ones by the intermittent throbbing of their engines - or so I thought.

We had been in this cottage only two days when we found the dog was missing. This worried my mother for she feared he might be causing trouble like chasing sheep. However, after about twelve hours, a message was brought to us about him. He had been found sitting on the front doorstep of the old house very early in the morning. It was amazing how he had found his way for he had been taken by car when our removal took place. He was brought back safely. Then once more Nigger was in trouble. One evening just outside our front gate he had a fight with a dog twice his size. Someone parted them. Nigger ended up with a damaged ear. At this point my mother decided she must let him go. He was used to country life not busy roads and built-up areas. However, we found a home for him with my sister in Crowland. He didn't reign there for long for after he'd killed some turkeys they decided they must have him put to sleep before he caused any more damage.

Since our new house was so small - two rooms up and two

down - I was given a shed in the garden for my workshop. This was quite a comfortable place in which to work. There was one large window along the whole of one side for which my mother had made a pretty cotton curtain. There was also a coke stove for heating, my work table with the knitting machine, and room for winding my wool. A table under the window served a useful purpose for pressing my completed work. I had by now the use of a gas iron for pressing. My mother would sometimes bring in her sewing in the afternoons. She had more time to sit and relax now most of the family had married and moved elsewhere to live. There were just my mother, myself, and a young sister still at school. It was usual for me to start work early and to finish early. I was rather afraid of working out in the shed after dark. This arrangement went very well for several months, working in the shed during the day and finishing off my work by the fire in our small kitchen in the evening.

About six months later we were offered a council house in Spalding Common further down the same road. This house was much larger and more convenient. We moved in and the shed was transferred to the new garden. We were very satisfied and everything seemed to sail along nicely. There was plenty of room for me to do my work but, alas, one afternoon in the December gales I was sitting at my knitting machine working when I heard a tremendous roar followed by several crashes. Thinking I had been hit by a bomb I just waited for the end. My mother and all the neighbours ran out to see what had happened. The gale had taken the roof of the shed right off and, luckily for me, perhaps because I was sitting down at the time, the roof just missed me as it passed over my head and crashed to the ground in front of me. Someone damped down the fire in the small stove as the wind could easily have caused a bad blaze. The shed was a complete write-off. From then on the spare bedroom was made into a workroom for me. It was heated by a small paraffin stove. This was to be my workroom for the next eight years.

I often worked late in the evenings. The Home Workers' Scheme provided me with several large school orders. Quite often I would be given an order for ten dozen pairs of boys' school stockings, sometimes grey with two navy stripes in the turned-down tops. I was paid one shilling per pair for the labour: they sent me the wool. As time passed I got the idea of making ladies' ribbed stockings in Clark's stranded cotton. It took about thirty penny balls to make one pair of these stockings. The most difficult part was winding the cotton. A knot had to be tied to join each ball making sure all four strands had been included in the knot. These stockings were quite popular particularly as they didn't take coupons to produce. Some people liked them plain knit with clocks at the ankles. Others liked a narrow rib with shapings at the back of the leg. I charged four shillings a pair for the knitting, the customer buying the cotton which was obtainable in several shades. My idea was to save as much money as possible to help me one day to get right away from this soul-destroying occupation. I knew very well there was nothing I could do while the war lasted. Apart from the odd short visits to friends in Boston I got out very little during the war. If it had not been for the family helping out with the occasional joint when they killed a pig, and the few eggs from my sister's hens, we might have found our meagre rations hard to stretch through the week, but we did manage because of my mother's good management.

Although we could often hear the bombs dropping on distant towns all I can remember is the night bombs fell on Boston and Spalding, killing people and causing many fires. One incident I have not forgotten. The supervisor of the home workers had visited me one day to book my work and to be paid for wool purchased for my private work. He stayed at an hotel in West Street, Boston, for the night, visiting other home workers on the way. He had a very narrow escape for a bomb was dropped that night on the hotel and killed the proprietor's two young daughters. I remember that night being awakened by the neighbours outside calling that Spalding was on fire and my mother, who always slept in some of her underclothes during the war, was soon up and dressed going downstairs with the black handbag she kept ready containing her insurance papers and anything else of value. She always made sure it wasn't very far away when she retired for the night. I failed to get the point really for, should we have got a direct hit, it would have been destroyed anyway. I think that night was the most alarming for me.

By 1944 some lighting restrictions were partly lifted in certain parts of the country. How we looked forward to the end of hostilities when things would become normal again, but it didn't happen as suddenly as that even when war had ended. Rationing was to go on for years.

VE day was upon us and I remember my mother and I sitting in our living room at Spalding Common listening to the voice of Winston Churchill and his famous words, "Our dear Channel Islands are free again", and the thrill I felt as I thought of one of my Girl Guide friends who had married and gone to live in Jersey at he beginning of the war. I had often wondered how she was getting on during the German occupation. Some months later I had a letter from her. She had fared quite well. She and her husband ran a small farm. Everything of course had to be shared with the Germans. For additional food they used to dry seaweed in the sun and cook it.

There were celebrations for VE day and a tea for the old-age pensioners but my mother wouldn't join them in spite of all the persuading. She rarely would mix. However, she did make a cake for the occasion. In spite of the shortages she could make a very good sponge with dried egg and no fat. It was very tasty with home-made strawberry jam for the filling. The cakes on sale in the shops were rather dry and usually one had to queue for them. We were full of hope that the end of queueing for food was now in sight.

7.

AFTER THE WAR

1947 was a memorable year in the history of my old school. In early January of that year some of us travelled up to York to attend the inaugural meeting of the King's Manor Old Students Association (KMOSA). It was quite a thrill to be back in the old school and to meet some of the teachers again. It was decided at this meeting to hold a reunion every year. A committee was formed and we arranged the first reunion for the summer. This was the first time I had ventured away from home on my own. The trip involved my staying in York overnight. I stayed at the YWCA for bed and breakfast and for lunch on the following day, which was a Sunday.

It was a very pleasant experience for me and I met some very interesting women. One of them escorted me to the station and saw me on to my train. The weather was bitterly cold that weekend. There were no straight-through trains to Spalding on Sundays so my brother-in-law met me at Peterborough and drove me home to Spalding Common. It must have been the coldest journey I have ever experienced. The train was so crowded that I had to stand from York to Doncaster. It was good to be back home especially when we awoke the following morning to find thick snow and the forecasts promised more to come. This winter of 1947 turned out to be one of the worst. The snow hung about until April in the outlying districts. It had been piled high on both sides of the road mostly by Italian prisoners. Later in the spring we were faced with the prospect of flooding. The river was expected to burst its banks in the direction of Spalding Common. I remember my brother coming to carry our furniture upstairs. However, it turned out that the flooding went over the opposite side over Crowland. I remember hearing on the radio that the river banks were being reinforced by pushing old wartime tanks into the breaches.

1947 was not a very lucky year for me. I answered two advertisements for home teacher posts. One was with the London County Council. I was short-listed for this but the advertisement had not specified that a sighted person was required. The interview was straightforward. I answered all the questions put by the panel. They told me to wait. After the remaining applicants had disappeared from the waiting-room, I was called before the panel again and told I could have the job, but all that they could allow me towards the cost of a guide was ten shillings a week. As the salary was only three pounds a week and a guide would need at least half of that I knew that I would not be able to manage, and had to turn down the offer. I learned later that the person appointed, a sighted person, did not have the home teacher's certificate. It was then the practice for local authorities to take on uncertified teachers provided they secured the necessary qualifications within two years of their appointment.

The second interview took place in Gateshead. This was a very tiring journey on a cold and foggy day and must have cost the authority quite a lot in taxis and trains. After I arrived at the Town Hall nearly two hours late it was discovered that this post wasn't suitable for a blind person. The district in which the vacancy had occurred was a very busy one traffic-wise with buses, trolley buses, and a great deal of heavy traffic. However, all concerned were very helpful and someone saw me on to my train afterwards. Since it was realised that I could not do the return journey the same day I had to break the journey home, spend the night in Doncaster, and complete the journey to Spalding the next morning. A booking had been made for me for evening meal, bed, and breakfast at the Daneham Hotel which was a short taxi ride from the station. This was the first time I had stayed in a hotel. Everyone with whom I came into contact was most helpful. My meals were taken up to my room. I remember I did not sleep. I was a little bit scared with all the outside and inside noises. The maid had told me to push the bell button over the wash bowl if I required any help but I didn't. At least I didn't mean to! As I was washing the next morning I must have accidentally touched this button for a knock on my bedroom door startled me and the voice of the maid said: "Did you want something, Madam?" I had to apologise but I did feel rather foolish.

I arrived home again disappointed and yet, I am sure, wiser

for the experience. My mother worried although I had told her little white lies about someone meeting me on and off trains. I just would not be beaten. There must be a way of getting away from my soul-destroying job. I would write to the RNIB and ask for an interview. I had read in my Braille magazines that they ran courses for telephonists and shorthand-typists at their commercial college at Oldbury Grange in Shropshire. Telephony was a three months' course. As I had saved nearly £200 from knitting the stranded cotton stockings I could offer to pay my own expenses. I spoke of this idea to my mother who took a very gloomy view of it all. Nevertheless, I went ahead and applied for an interview for the telephony course. I explained that, if selected, I would be willing to pay my own fees. It wasn't easy getting letters written as I could not then type. Most of my correspondence, where possible, was done in braille. A date was fixed for the interview.

The journey to London was quite an easy one. I took a taxi from my home to Spalding station. Fares were very reasonable in those days and trains ran straight through from Spalding to King's Cross where the station staff saw me into a taxi. I arrived in the RNIB during the lunch hour. I was ushered into a corridor and given a chair to sit on to wait for my appointment at 2 o'clock. As I sat there waiting thoughts and doubts were chasing round in my head. I had got to make it as this was my only chance. As two o'clock approached people on their way back from lunch streamed past me. I remember someone poking my foot with his cane. Everybody seemed to be tapping their sticks. I hadn't yet carried one. I was too proud. Besides, what would my mother say? Someone escorted me into the interview room.

The panel consisted of three gentlemen and a lady. I was asked several questions, how to spell a few words, and given a hearing test. Numbers were whispered from a distance and I had to repeat them. I felt quite happy about the interview. It wasn't the ordeal I had expected. I was asked to wait outside and after a short time I was once more called into the interview room. I was told I had passed the interview but the panel suggested that I should be trained for shorthand and typing. That was something I had not thought myself capable of. It was a year's crash course and I could not possibly afford the fees for that long. I was told that I would be trained under the Ministry of Labour scheme. In addition I would receive an allowance of thirty-eight shillings a week. I would also be provided with railway vouchers to and from the college for holidays. All this sounded too good to be true. I just hoped I would be able to master both typing and shorthand at the age of forty. They also suggested I might find it easier if I carried a white cane to get the help I would need from the general public. This business of getting about alone had not yet quite sunk into my imagination but on my way out I called in to the showroom and there and then purchased a white cane, a sectional one. Some kind person took care of me and saw me back on to my train to Spalding. She also phoned my taxi driver to tell him what train I was on. How extremely kind and helpful people were! I shall never forget when I arrived back home in our small kitchen my mother looked at my folded white cane and asked me what I was going to do with that. When I told her I meant to find my way about with it she said, as always, that I would never manage alone.

Now I was accepted for training and was told that I would be hearing further from the Ministry of Labour. In due course one of their doctors came to examine me. He told me: "So far as your health is concerned you are in."

During the waiting period of about a month I became even more bored with the knitting machine. I had stopped knitting the stranded cotton stockings, only making up the wool I had in stock into outstanding orders and hoping every day I was making the last sock. Although I felt rather apprehensive about the whole idea I hoped I could learn all that one had to learn in the allotted time. My mother wasn't much help, always looking on the black side of things and saying I would never get about alone. If I never went about alone in my home town how could I manage in a strange town? I didn't intend trying to get around with a white stick in Spalding where I was so well known but I meant to have a good try when I got away. I felt rather bad at leaving my mother. I don't suppose I could have left her were it not that my youngest sister was still at home.

Eventually my railway voucher arrived and the day came for my journey to the commercial college, Bridgnorth, Shropshire. With some help from friends I had got the journey all mapped out in my mind. It was quite a challenge. To put her mind at rest, I had to tell my mother that someone would be helping me to change trains. Firstly I took a taxi to the station and then a train to Peterborough North where I had to change for Peterborough East. This change was an easy one in those days for a waiting train took me to the East station. The next train took me to Rugby where I had to change for Birmingham New Street. There I learned that I must get from New Street to Snowhill station. Since it was only a short walk away someone escorted me there and on to the train for Kidderminster where I had to change for Bridgnorth. This was a diesel train and was the first of its kind in which I had ever ridden. It sounded more like a bus and rattled a bit. I was met at Bridgnorth station by the warden and her assistant who took me to the college by car.

It was late afternoon when we reached the college. Someone gave me a very welcome cup of tea. I hadn't had a drink all day. It isn't easy for a visually-handicapped person travelling on their own to find cafes or coffee stalls on stations nor on the train whether or not there is a buffet car. I had yet to learn about these things. After this rather traumatic journey I learned there was an easier way by travelling via Wolverhampton. That way I should have had fewer changes.

The college atmosphere at Oldbury Grange was so different from that of my first day at school. The students with whom I came into contact gave me the impression that hard work was the centre of everything. Indeed it had to be to get through the course in the allotted time. It didn't take me long to get into the swim. I had to learn all the shorthand signs by heart. I found I could memorise them by learning from my braille copy of the shorthand system in bed under the bedclothes at night. As well as learning all day I had to put in time after tea in the evenings. In the mornings it was shorthand practice. This worried me for I found that the actual operation of the shorthand machime was so different from the ordinary writing on the braille frame to which I had always been accustomed. The shorthand machine is operated by means of six keys and a space bar.

I found typing very fascinating and right from the start was anxious to learn. I remember after I'd worked through all the lessons in the typing manual how glad and interested I was when the instructor allowed me to go on to tabulations. We were given a lesson to work out and type and as soon as we completed that perfectly we went on to the next and more complicated one. The first exercise had only one column of figures and we progressed to six or more columns some with complicated headings. We had to work out the number of spaces in each column and the number of spaces in the headings and split them up in order to fit the column. The tabulation keys had then to be set before one could get on with the typing. It could take quite a long time to work out the columns.

The sighted typist doesn't have the same problem for she can see exactly where the tabulations should be placed. I found I enjoyed all the typing lessons and put in as much practice as I could. I didn't look forward with quite the same zest to the short-hand lessons. I could memorise all the signs. When I was in college there were over 900 word signs and over 100 group signs. There were also quite a number of phrase signs. What bothered me most was the operation of the shorthand machine. When one is doing a speed test there isn't time to think which way up a letter goes. If one wrote the letter F as on the braille frame it turned out to be the letter J on the shorthand machine. It was not easy but I knew that I would master the problem eventually.

After all the hard work during the week we relaxed a little at weekends. On occasional Friday evenings there was a dance at the college. The dining room was cleared of tables. Some of the RAF from the nearby camp were invited. They danced with students and staff under the watchful eye of their commanding officer of course and of our own warden and her deputy. They were all too young for me. Sometimes during the weekend we students would go out for a meal in the evening to a rather nice restaurant in the old part of Bridgnorth. On other occasions we would have tea and fancy cakes at Jones' cafe.

I was by now becoming quite used to my white stick. Although I was usually with other blind people I found the stick gave me a lot of confidence. There were some very pleasant walks round about Oldbury Grange. Some parts were quite hilly. One had to climb quite a steep hill, Panpudding Hill, to get into Bridgnorth. After the flatness of Lincolnshire I found my legs were terribly stiff and achy for the first few days. However, it did wear off and then I simply did not notice the hills.

It was quite normal practice to take short walks before break-fast or just after lunch. I remember one afternoon after lunch taking the warden's dog, Shelley, for a few minutes' walk. We had walked along the road for several minutes when to my horror

Shelley gave a jerk, pulled his lead out of my hand and disappeared out of my hearing. After being trusted with him I hardly dare return without him. When I did arrive back in great distress I knocked on the warden's door and confessed that I had lost Shelley. I need not have been so upset for Shelley was lying safely in his basket and had been for several minutes.

My bedroom on the first floor I shared with three others. The age ranges were twenty-three, mid twenties, thirty-two, and myself, aged forty. The youngest had only recently left Chorleywood College. The thirty-two-year-old had served in the Land Army during the war and was fast losing her sight. She was doing the telephony course and finding braille quite a challenge. The other girl, who was quite young, was the daughter of a Devon doctor and did well on the typing course.

At that time the typing students outnumbered the telephony students. As their course was only for three months they were coming and going all the time. Some of them were well over forty and some had only recently lost their sight. Some were already in a job and their firms were taking them back again as telephonists after the course. One man had been a master in a boys' school for many years, had lost his sight, had been rehabilitated at the RNIB centre at Torquay and was now taking a telephony course. Most students were very young, some of them having just left school or college. Some had been blind all their lives.

At the beginning of my second term there was a new intake of typists. Others, after completing the course, had left and were very soon found jobs by RNIB placement officers. Although the majority of these new students were quite young there was one student, more or less like myself, who had been working with a knitting machine for some years. She had been brought up in Dr. Barnado's home until school age. She found the course rather exacting but came through. I got to know her through the warden asking me to take her out with me; she said I would be good for her. However she managed to get around quite as well as I did, if not better.

Quite near to the college I found the small church which I was to attend on Sunday evenings. More often than not I was accompanied by one or more of my friends. On one occasion we were taken to Hanley to hear their choral society in Handel's Messiah. I haven't forgotten it to this day: it was so beautiful.

This second term was a very wet and cold one with lots of snow in February but we did manage to get out for our Saturday evening meal. We were paid our thirty-eight shillings allowance every Friday and enjoyed it to the full. I must say that the food at the college was very good and plentiful. It was interesting to sit in the lounge listening to all the different dialects - Welsh, Cockney, West Country, Birmingham, and the Midlands. The school was open for about two hours during the evenings and several of us took advantage of this. It was apart from the actual house. To get there one had to walk along a gravel path. On dark nights this was rather scary when there was a gale blowing. Usually other people besides myself would be going across. One evening there seemed to be nobody else going so I braved it alone. I entered the typing room and sat down at my desk to type a paper. All was quiet and I believed I was alone in the room. I was typing away merrily when I heard a rustling behind me. Then I heard three taps on my desk and a voice saying, "Hilda, is it dibble or dabble?" I jumped and said "What?" The voice said: "Is it audible or audable?" I hadn't heard the young man enter the room. He did often ask me the spelling of words. He gave me quite a shock although there wasn't anything to be afraid of as people and staff were working in other rooms in the building.

It was about the end of my second term that my worries about the progress of my shorthand became real. The typing instructor had seen the report of the shorthand instructor. It wasn't good. My shorthand speed had not improved as well as it should have done although my typing work was quite satisfactory. There was a folder with all my work to prove it. The thoughts of the knitting machine loomed up in my mind. However, the typing teacher seemed to want to help in some way. He suggested I do just dicta-phone typing. The Ministry of Labour would have to be consulted about this as they were financing my course.

The next afternoon he allowed me to leave the class twenty minutes early to go to the Ministry of Labour office in Bridgnorth to put my problems to the manager there and to show him the folder with all my perfect work. Fortunately by this time I could find my way about quite well. When I reached the office, with a little help, I was shown into the manager's office and told to sit down. I explained my dilemma and asked if I might be allowed to switch from shorthand to dictaphone. He didn't see why not but said he would have to get in touch with the RNIB to ask for their approval. After a few days I was told that I could transfer to dictaphone typing. At that time the college did not have dictaphones so the typing instructor took me over to a firm in Wolverhampton for a morning's work on the dictaphone. He was quite satisfied with my performance and felt sure that I would manage this machine alright. I was offered another chance at shorthand, if I wished, but declined at this stage dreading another failure. I was pleased that the situation had been saved for the moment. I did not take failure at all well and was always a bad loser: I still am. I would study the subject of shorthand in my spare time with a view to taking evening classes later. Now I was to spend all my school time with typing.

I was working for my first examination, the Elementary RSA. The speed for this was 30 words per minute.

About a fortnight before the examination Miss Thompson from Homes Department of the RNIB came to interview me. She asked me, if I should be successful in the forthcoming examination, would I like to take a job straight away rather than finish the year's course. I agreed that I would like to be in a job and gain real typing experience. I also told her that I intended to pursue shorthand at evening classes.

The day of the typing examination came round. I don't think I have ever felt more nervous but I did manage to complete the accuracy test at the required thirty words per minute. I didn't quite finish the long paper containing some tabulations but I had demonstrated how to set it out and I had started the tabulations. This paper had been dictated to me on the shorthand machine at a slow speed which enabled me to write it in longhand so that I could read it easily. I felt I must have failed as I hadn't quite finished. I was so utterly miserable that I didn't want my evening meal but went to my bedroom and cried my eyes out. The thought of failure was bad enough but the prospect of returning to my old job was even worse.

In due course the examination results were issued and I had secured a pass. I was disappointed for I had aimed at a distinction. However, I was relieved that I wasn't disqualified altogether. With this news I heard that I had a job to go to and accommodation in a hostel in London. The job was with G.P.O. H.Q. and I would receive dictaphone training at the Treasury training school. I was to leave the college in a fortnight. It was now spring and very pleasant were the walks through the lanes. My worries were over for the time being at any rate.

The Saturday previous to my leaving for London we went to Jones' cafe for cream cakes and tea, a sort of farewell do. I had made several friends some of whom I met in London later and to this day we still keep up a correspondence.

It came to the day of my departure. The journey to London was a much easier one this time. Someone saw me on to the train at Wolverhampton and I think there was only one change. I certainly found that, while carrying a white stick, I got all the help possible. In fact this help continued for the next twenty years while I travelled up and down to my home town. I became familiar with the layout of King's Cross station and discovered how easy it was on the tube from the mainline station to Bayswater underground. From there I had about ten minutes' walk along Moscow Road, turning left into Palace Court and to the hostel which was to be my home for several years.

8.

LONDON, INDEPENDENCE, AND ERIC

I was greeted at the hostel by the warden. She escorted me up four flights of stairs to my room which I was to share with Eunice Woodget, a very charming and talented girl of twenty-three. It was quite a large room which looked out on to the street - Palace Court. My bed was under the window.

We each had our own chest of drawers and a wardrobe. There was a gas fire if required and we took turns to insert the shilling necessary for about two hours' heat. There were two easy chairs and a folding table. The room was well carpeted. Just off one corner of the room was a walk-in cupboard in which was a wash-bowl, several shelves, and a stand for a gas ring and kettle. We were allowed to make hot drinks during the evenings and at weekends if we wished. I was given two cups and saucers and a teapot. Since tea and sugar were still on ration we were given our portions by the warden. We could also have some milk after the evening meal to take upstairs. I think this was the beginning of my independence - when I could have my own cup, saucer, and teapot. Later I can remember buying myself some nice china cups and saucers in Shepherd's Bush market.

We could entertain our friends in our rooms at weekends. Sharing with another person meant there had to be a bit of give and take. My room mate and I didn't ever seem to clash and managed to fit in. I went home at least once a month. As her home was only a few miles away in Kent she got away very often.

We took breakfast and evening meal in the dining-room and all meals at weekends. Breakfast was fairly early for we all had to get tubes or buses to work. Most of us had to be at work by nine o'clock and the RNIB workers by 8.30.

Each one of us was given a latch key to the front door. In

the hall was a block of small pigeon holes in which our mail was put along with a card which had our name and pigeon hole number in print and braille. When we left the house we placed our card on the hall table. Whenever we returned we replaced the card in our pigeonhole. When we came home in the evening and found no other cards left on the table, indicating that everyone was in, we then locked the front door.

When I arrived at the hostel I was told I had an appointment for an interview at the Treasury training school for tuition on the dictaphone. As this was not for a further week the RNIB allowed me to work in their office for a few days. This was my first intro- duction to office work. I don't think I did much work, maybe a few letters, but it was certainly more interesting than just hanging about at the hostel and I was able to meet people. That week I didn't earn anything so I didn't pay any board.

When the day came for my interview at the Treasury I was escorted there by the RNIB placements officer. The 'Controller of Typists' interviewed me and accepted me as a trainee for the dictaphone. (It is now called audio.) I was offered a job in the Treasury typing pool on completion of the training as they trained only for their own department. On the advice of the placements officer I was very happy to accept and had to turn down the original offer of a job in the G.P.O. H.Q. I was astonished at being offered two jobs after all the years of waiting. At that time in 1948 there was a demand for blind typists. All the people I had met in training at the college in Bridgnorth seemed to get jobs quickly when they finished their training.

I enjoyed the week's dictaphone training and found everyone so helpful. Everyday at lunch-time there was always someone willing to take me under their wing. After lunch they often took me for walks in St. James' Park or along the Embankment. They also helped me mobility-wise by showing me where to find the shops, the post office, tube stations, and restaurants. The work in training didn't worry me very much as it was fairly straightforward as soon as I got used to the dictaphone. I think I found more diffi- culty in the actual job with hearing what was said. Some voices were not very distinct until one got familiar with the work. Of course one could always backspace and listen to the phrase again but if one backspaced too often on the same bit it became worn and harder to hear.

At last came the day I had been longing for. I had to report to the Treasury door at nine o'clock on Monday where someone met me and escorted me to the typing pool. The supervisor introduced me to the girls and showed me to my desk just behind the door. I don't know if this desk was chosen for me to help in my efforts at getting about or whether it was just a coincidence that I was near to the door. It was a help not to have to plod through rows of desks when leaving or entering the room.

On my desk was an Imperial typewriter complete with the braille scale; a dictaphone machine stood on the floor at one side. Later I had a Phillips' machine which stood on the desk. There were four drawers in the desk in which to keep typing paper of various sizes as well as various types of envelope. There were several kinds of paper – semi-official, official, air mail, Northern Ireland, and DATAC (Development Area Trade Advisory Committee). As years went on other types of paper came along. Then there was minute paper, plain paper, flimsies for copies, and carbon paper. Until I could remember how I had arranged all this in the desk I marked each pile in braille. No one ever disturbed any of the paper during my time. One got to know the feel of the different papers. The paper headings felt slightly raised in most cases. I don't remember ever getting a sheet of headed notepaper upside down. Then we were shown just where the reference should go. We counted the number of lines to turn up and the number of spaces along and kept a braille note with the relevant paper. I don't think I did much work on my first morning. By the time I had got all the different papers organised in my desk drawers, signed the Official Secrets Act, which the supervisor read to me, it was time for lunch. Most of the girls brought sandwiches. Since I would be having a big meal in the evening at the hostel I bought either sandwiches or rolls from the trolley which went round at lunchtimes. Someone would always make a cup of tea or coffee if required.

After lunch on this my first day at work I was given a job. This first job was two short minutes, easy to hear and quite straightforward. When all the typewriters were going the noise was quite deafening. I was amazed at the speed at which some of the girls typed. I knew I would never reach that speed. They were all sighted and could correct their mistakes. They were so experienced that they could keep up with the dictaphone whereas I listened to a sentence, switched off my machine, and then typed what I had just heard. I could not type and listen to the machine at the same time. I tried to be as accurate as possible because someone else would have to spend time in correcting my mistakes.

On Friday afternoons we received our wages. In those days we had to queue up for this. I remember the feeling of pride when given my first pay packet. It contained the princely sum of five pounds and that evening I paid to the warden of our hostel my fee of three pounds.

As the summer went by I began to occupy my thoughts with the prospect of joining evening classes for shorthand and enrolled in early September at the Westminster College of Commerce. This first winter I intended to work for a speed of eighty words per minute, and, if considered up to it, wanted to sit the R.S.A. examination sometime in March. I attended college two nights a week. Sometimes I felt so tired after a day in the office that I could very easily have gone to sleep. I simply must put all I had got into this because, if successful, I would be upgraded to the shorthand-typing pool. It also meant more pay. Attending evening classes meant missing my evening meal at the hostel. If required we could have sandwiches which would be in our pigeonholes when we arrived home. We took these to our rooms where we could always make a hot drink. On days like this I had lunch out at mid-day. I practised my shorthand during the evening. My room companion was most helpful in dictating to me from braille some shorthand speeds.

And so the weeks flew by. March came round and the shorthand examination. I was well rewarded when I received notice that I had gained my RSA certificate for 80 w.p.m. This resulted in my being transferred and upgraded to shorthand-typist grade II. I found this much more interesting. How good it was having an actual person dictating the work and not just a voice through a headphone, and in my opinion much easier to understand. How things have improved in audio typing since those days!

The next winter I enrolled again at the college for my 100 w.p.m. in order to be upgraded to first class grade I. I had already obtained the intermediate typing certificate RSA. This was another fairly hard-working winter in the evenings but I did want to become grade I to improve my pay which wasn't all that good in those days.

In March 1950 I was successful in the RSA shorthand examination at 100 w.p.m. which meant I had reached my grade I typist's status. That year I also completed my probationary period and became an established civil servant. I felt on top of the world knowing that I was in a permanent post at last. I didn't join any evening classes the next winter for shorthand. However, I was working in my own time for the 120 w.p.m. which would entitle me to a proficiency allowance.

About that time my department was running a quarter-of-an-hour speed test at 120 w.p.m. every morning at nine. I took advantage of these short classes which were quite popular.

Once a month I visited my mother for the weekend. I left work at five o'clock, took the 77 bus to King's Cross, and caught a train round about six o'clock to Spalding. In those days one could book a seat on the train for one shilling. During the lunch hour on that Friday I would call into the railway office in Whitehall to purchase my ticket and book a corner seat facing the engine. It was advisable to book a seat as the train was usually crowded.

Our taxi man at Spalding met me and my mother was always waiting for me with a nice hot meal. I returned to London on the Sunday evening and with help down to the tube I could be in the hostel just before ten o'clock. Travelling at Christmas was rather hectic. I used to book a seat on two trains in case I missed the first one. This happened only once so far as I can remember. As I usually did, I took the 77 bus from Whitehall to King's Cross, someone helped me to a seat on the platform and asked a porter to tell me when the train came in. I sat waiting. I heard over the loudspeaker that the next train on this platform was calling at Leicester and numerous other stations. That was the wrong direction for me so I rose clutching handbag, suitcase, and white stick and called to a passerby that I required some help. A porter very soon put me right. I had been waiting on the King's Cross suburban station. I caught the second train on which I had a booked seat.

On another occasion I went wrong on my way back. The train was rather late. We had stopped at the usual places and I assumed the next stop would be King's Cross. When the train stopped at the next station, and it sounded as if people were getting off, I picked up my belongings and followed the crowd off the train. The people just seemed to disappear. I knew at once that it wasn't

King's Cross. It was too quiet. However a kindly porter came to my help and told me that I was at Finsbury Park. He saw me on to the next train to King's Cross. Since it was getting late – well after ten – I didn't get off the tube at Bayswater station as I didn't fancy Moscow Road late at night but went on to the next station – Notting Hill Gate. I happened to be lucky there for it was a policeman who helped me out of the station. When I told him I was going to the hostel in Palace Court he escorted me all the way and handed me over to the warden. He had pressed the doorbell before I had a chance to produce my latch key.

As I visited my home so regularly I did not often go anywhere else for a holiday. The snag was that when travelling on Friday evenings I had to take the Saturday morning as annual leave. We worked on Saturday mornings in those days and these weekends did eat into my leave allowance. It was much better after 1956 when the five–day–week arrived. Then I sometimes took a day's leave on the Monday to extend the weekend at home.

Now that I didn't have to attend evening classes for shorthand I thought I would embark on pastures new. I enrolled at the City Literary Institute for one evening class a week. I decided on speech development and voice production. These classes were most enjoyable as poetry and drama were just what I wanted and a great relaxation after the day's work. At school I had found Shakespeare boring but these classes helped to give me a better understanding of the writer and his works. I also attended some interesting lectures at the 'City Lit.'

I became a member of the London Sports' Club for the Blind. Every Tuesday evening we met in St. Peter's school, in Lower Belgrave Street, Victoria. We learned ballroom dancing and played chess and dominoes etc. Once a month there was a whist drive with braille cards. I had never played whist before and looked forward to this evening. There were rambles in the spring and summer organised by the sports club, usually about every third Sunday. We would meet at one of the London stations and go out by train to a given point. We would walk in the countryside, keeping off the main roads, through fields or woods and up hills. I remember we climbed Box Hill more than once. After a lot of rain the hills and slopes were very muddy and we sometimes arrived back with very muddy shoes. It was all part of the fun. The sports club also held a monthly dance on a Saturday evening in the YWCA in Great Russell Street. Now that I had not to study so hard I liked to use my evenings for recreation. During the summer evenings a band played in Hyde Park which was almost on our doorstep.

The summer of 1951 proved to be rather varied. I was still working for my 120 w.p.m. shorthand examination. I hadn't yet achieved the speed and still needed a great deal of practice. However I sat the typing proficiency test and was successful. With it came an increase in pay which was always welcome.

During the summer of that year I met the man I was to marry later. The chain of events which led up to this were rather unusual. It happened that one Saturday morning Eric walked up to the flower seller lady at Piccadilly Circus and asked her if she knew of any organisation for the blind he could contact with a view to helping blind students with their studies, such as reading to them or acting as an escort for walks or to concerts at weekends. I learned later that he had an urge to help someone less fortunate than himself as he felt he was leading a rather selfish existence.

His work as an Administrative Engineer at EMI was interesting and successful. He was a bachelor in his early forties and lived in Middlesex. The old flower seller suggested he contact the RNIB which, she was sure, could help him. She even told him which bus to take telling him to hurry as the RNIB closed half day on Saturdays. They directed him to our hostel where there were telephony students on a short-term stay before being posted. He arrived at the hostel and found that the warden couldn't think of anyone needing help as most of the guests went their various ways at weekends. As he left to catch his bus back she suddenly had a thought and followed him. Just as he was about to board the bus she called him back and told him of a young telephonist, a man in his early twenties, whom he might be able to help in some way.

At weekends and evenings he came to the hostel to take one or other person for a walk or to help them in their studies by reading to them. It was some weeks before I really came into contact with him. We often passed each other in the hall with perhaps the odd "good morning" or "good evening". That was as far as things went. I was attending a series of cookery classes at an evening school in Bath Street, off Old Street in the East End. This class was on Thursday evenings. I was rushing along the Bayswater Road one Thursday evening to get the bus when I met him going along to the hostel. He asked me if I needed any help. I declined as I always managed. That was the first time we had spoken apart from casual greetings in the hall. The outward journey wasn't too difficult. There was no problem on the return journey either for someone from the class would always help. It did happen very occasionally that the bus took me beyond my stop. When this happened to me during the evening I got in a panic as there were not so many people around after nine o'clock. It was much better after ten o'clock when the theatre and other places of entertainment were emptying. I didn't like the tubes in these quiet times. I remember getting off the train at Bayswater station one evening and standing on the platform expecting to get the usual help to the lift. Nobody got off except myself. The train pulled away and I think I was the only person on the platform. I just found the wall and waited for the next train to come in. It was really ghostly quiet. I couldn't even hear a porter about. At last I did hear a voice. Someone was coming down to the platform – I could hear the hum of the lift. The lift attendant rescued me. My fears were over. Even now I have dreams of getting lost. It was easier on the buses as there was usually the conductor to help.

I would often go for a walk in Hyde Park after our evening meal with a friend, Irene Churchill, whom I had met at evening classes. She sometimes invited me to her home for the weekend. I enjoyed this very much. I found these weekends with René and her parents more relaxing than the weekends spent at home with my mother. My couple of days at home were largely spent helping in whatever ways I could and I got very little rest. Also there was the trauma of the train journeys on my own. After my young sister married and left home I felt anxious and worried about leaving my mother all alone. In fact I had given this a lot of thought and had had my name included on a transfer list for a post in a government office in the Spalding area. It would have been a sacrifice for I was enjoying my life in London and by now I had made a good circle of friends. I hadn't yet quite reached my goal in the shorthand proficiency. For the first time in my life I began to feel that I was living at the top of my capacity, albeit at rather a late age. If a transfer to a post in my home town had come along I should have had to think of my mother first. However the transfer never came.

One Saturday morning while I was having lunch the warden

85

told me that Eric would be coming and that there was nobody for him to take out or help. She wondered if I needed any help. I remember thinking that I did not need any assistance just then. Then it suddenly dawned on me that I was intending to go to King's Cross station to buy a ticket and book a seat on a train to York the following Friday evening. I was to attend my old school reunion and meet an old friend. We were expecting to have dinner on the train and stay overnight at an hotel close to the old school. I agreed I might be glad of some help although I had done this on my own several times. When Eric rang the doorbell and the warden introduced me I could not change my mind and the offer was gratefully accepted.

This weekend my friends were calling to take me home with them and had arranged to pick me up at five p.m. I left a message at the hostel asking them to wait should they arrive before I returned although I was sure there was plenty of time as it wasn't yet two o'clock. We took the tube to King's Cross which was quite a short journey. When I had finished my business there, since it was still quite early and a lovely day, Eric suggested that we walk back and we ended up walking through Hyde Park. Remembering that I had said my friends were calling to take me for the weekend Eric wondered if he could be of any assistance on my return journey to save them a journey. When he put the idea to my friends, thinking we knew each other well, they said they would be glad of his help and invited him for tea the next day saying that he could escort me back afterwards.

The following day, Sunday, was a beautiful summer day and we were all in the garden. At about four o'clock I heard footsteps on the garden path coming towards the lawn and a voice saying he'd rung the doorbell and got no reply so he had taken the liberty of looking for us round the back. He was soon given a deck chair and made welcome. We were to have tea in the garden on this glorious day. My friends went into the house to prepare tea and they asked me to entertain our guest for a few minutes.

There have been times when I have been lost for words, and this was one of them. I remember trying to start a conversation by saying "What a lovely day". His reply was "What a lovely lady". I did not know how to follow that remark. The tea trolley appeared and we were all soon tucking into sandwiches, cakes, and cups of tea. This was what I loved, having tea outside in good weather.

These weekends with my friends were so enjoyable. I was completely spoiled and I loved it. I remember nearly every detail about their home. My bedroom, for instance, had a soft white carpet which was heavenly to walk on in bare feet.

After our tea party on the lawn we left for Bayswater. Before leaving me at my door Eric wondered if he could be of any further help in the evenings during the week. I thought of the journey to my cookery class on Thursday evenings and accepted his offer.

9.

ERIC

On the following Thursday Eric met me and escorted me to my cookery class. On the Friday evening I went straight to King's Cross from work and caught a train to York to attend the old students' reunion. A friend joined me on the train where we had dinner, which helped to pass away the time. After an enjoyable weekend at the school we returned on the Sunday afternoon. Eric had arranged to meet me at the station. He wanted to take me somewhere for a meal so we decided to take the 73 bus to Marble Arch and went to Lyons' Corner House. He found a table for two with waiter service. While we were talking over an excellent meal he wondered if I would like to go to Windsor the following Sunday. As I had never been there I accepted his offer.

I saw him the following Thursday for my cookery class as usual. On Sunday he turned up about ten o'clock and we made our way to Windsor. We must have walked miles through Windsor Great Park. I can remember hundreds of Boy Scouts marching through the town. We were most impressed by the rhythm of their steps. I think it must have been a special occasion as there were so many of them. We lunched at a rather nice pub - I forget the name now - and arrived back at the hostel in the early evening after a very interesting and enjoyable day. We planned to go out again when the weather was good. I remember on several occasions taking the underground to Epping and walking through the forest finishing up with lunch at the Wake Arms. How I looked forward to the weekends!

In those days we often had a meal out on Friday evenings. We visited many of the well-known restaurants round about. On Saturday evenings we went to a show. I think one of the first was *Perchance to Dream* by Ivor Novello. During the summer we often went to the Promenade concerts. This was the dawning of my taste for classical music.   Previously I had preferred the lighter side of music.   Eric believed that to be able to appreciate a piece of music one must listen to it over and over again.   His collection of records showed that Haydn and Beethoven were his favourites.   His hobbies were many and varied.   He read to me quite a lot, especially during the winter when we didn't get out so often.

I went home for my usual weekends once a month.   In October, while on one of these weekends, I decided to tell my mother about Eric.   I received no encouragement from her.   She thought I was quite alright as I was and that I would never manage a home of my own.   She was so much against this that I let the matter drop and did not mention it again.

About the end of November we talked about becoming engaged at Christmas.   I thought of the Christmas break and of being parted from each other for so long, so I wrote to my mother telling her our news.   I asked her if I could take Eric home with me to meet the family at Christmas.   I also said that if I could not take him home with me I would not be going home myself.   I am glad to say that my mother relented and said she would be pleased to see us at Christmas.

My celebrations began the Sunday before Christmas when I was taken to the Royal Albert Hall to hear Christmas carols in the afternoon.   I invited Eric back to the hostel for tea where I told my room companion that we had become engaged and were going to my home for Christmas.   The secret was out by now anyway - I was proud of my diamond ring.   After tea we went to Trafalgar Square to sing carols round the Christmas tree and hear the choirs singing on the steps of St. Martin-in-the-Fields.   The weather was cold and crisp and I remember walking back through Oxford Street and Marble Arch.   We called in at the Cumberland Hotel for a drink.   I understand there were Christmas trees and bright lights everywhere.   We were invited to several Christmas parties, including the office party.   It was a frantic week and during the lunch hours I was busy shopping for last-minute gifts.   Unfortunately we could not meet during the lunch hours as Eric's office was too far away from the West End.   Although I had managed on my own for so long I must say it was much easier having someone to guide me.

However, this exciting week soon passed and the day arrived

for the Christmas break. It was the day before Christmas Eve. I remember Eric meeting me off the 77 bus at King's Cross. What a relief to have his help for the crowds were terrific! Hitherto I had done this journey on my own, usually carrying suitcase, handbag, white stick, and other odd parcels. I sometimes think about this and wonder how I managed. I couldn't possibly have coped without all the help I got from the station staff and the general public. Help was always there if needed. I always accept help for I feel that if one turns down an offer the helper may not offer to help others in need. Once or twice I have had to struggle to stay on course if some kind soul wanted to take me across the road when I didn't really want to go. On the whole I did manage to make people understand where I wanted to be.

We were at last in the train bound for Spalding. As we sped along my mind was full of thoughts about the reception Eric would receive from my mother. Whatever her reaction it couldn't alter our decision. I hoped that she would approve.

When we arrived home my mother greeted us at the front door. It was good to be in our warm kitchen with a blazing fire and a smell of mince pies cooking and the kettle singing on the hook over the fire. After a meal my mother and young sister, Eric, and myself sat round the fire talking. I felt better now for I felt sure my mother and Eric would get along fine.

The following day, Christmas Eve, was a busy one. Eric helped my mother in every way he could. He insisted on going out to do the last-minute shopping. He helped with the washing up. My mother worked hard herself and liked to see everyone else pulling their weight.

Christmas Day 1951. For me it was the happiest Christmas since the loss of my father. We spent the morning in the kitchen opening presents and helping my mother with the preparations for lunch. In the afternoon Eric and I went out for a long walk. This was new ground for him as he had never visited Lincolnshire before. The rest of the day was spent at home with my mother and sister.

We had to return to London on Boxing Day as both of us had to start work again the following morning. I somehow felt that Eric had made a good impression on my mother and that he had been well accepted by the family. In the train on the return journey we talked about marriage. This of course would not be possible until we had found accommodation not too far from my place of work.

In late January 1952 Eric saw an advertisement in a shop window in Notting Hill, 'Bedsitter to let in Ossington Street'. This street was quite near the hostel and couldn't have been in a more convenient position for my bus to work. Eric went along in answer to the advertisement. The landlady asked him to call again as she had other people to interview. I think she must have phoned him asking him to take me along too. He was prepared to take the room and pay the rent for a few weeks until we could marry. As we had also got our names on the LCC housing list through the blind welfare, a bedsitter was just a temporary measure until a flat came our way. We managed to get the bedsitter and Eric moved in. The room was on the second floor, up four flights of stairs. This didn't bother me for I had to climb four flights of stairs at the hostel. The room was very large and airy with the window overlooking the street. It was nicely furnished and there were a gas fire and cooking facilities as well as a wash basin with hot and cold water. The landlady had seen me many times pass the top of the street on my way to work. We felt we could now go ahead with the wedding arrangements. We decided to go home the next weekend to see the vicar of my parish in Spalding. It was a mad rush to get everything done in a short weekend but we saw the vicar and filled in the necessary forms.

Saturday, 15th March, was the day appointed for the wedding. I think one should reside in the parish for a time before marriage but the fact that I had visited my home frequently over the years was accepted. My mother agreed to hold the wedding reception at home. I marvel even to this day how we managed to accommodate everyone. The buffet was to be laid out along one side of our front room. The caterers were booked. Since eggs were still on ration my family helped out with sufficient eggs for the cake – a three-tier square cake, just what I had wished for. The wedding was only six weeks away and we planned to spend a weekend at my home to hear the banns read out in church.

The 1st March fell on a Saturday. We travelled down on the Saturday afternoon and spent the weekend in Spalding putting the finishing touches to the wedding arrangements. We attended the parish church on Sunday morning to hear the banns and also saw the vicar about the wedding service. On Monday we finalised the arrangements and returned to London in the evening. The time seemed to pass so quickly when we were together but seemed endless at work. I found it difficult to concentrate on my work before the wedding especially on some of the more technical jobs.

I was told that I was entitled to a week's marriage leave and Eric took a week of his leave entitlement. We wanted to conserve some leave for a holiday in the summer. The Saturday before the wedding some friends went with me to D. H. Evans in Oxford Street to help me choose my outfit. We decided on a turquoise dress and a small feathery hat to match. I also chose a pink coat for going away afterwards. The accessories were silver grey. We ended the afternoon at a small tea shop in Queensway where we indulged in tea and cream cakes.

On Friday evening I travelled down to my home. Eric with his best man and friends followed later. I was greeted at the gate by my mother and sister. My sister and one of my nieces were to be my bridesmaids the following day.

Next morning, 15th March, we were all about early. How tensed up I felt wondering if everything would pass off according to plan. People seemed to be coming and going all the morning. The first to arrive were the bouquets and buttonholes. Then the caterers came with the food and the wedding cake. Family started to arrive. People were milling around upstairs and downstairs. My mother in her usual calm way was making sure that everything was in order. The day was a typical windy March day, happily with plenty of sunshine.

The wedding was scheduled for three o'clock to allow time for people from a distance to get there. The cars were at the house just before three to take us to the parish church, only a very short distance away. As I came out to get in the car someone sang *Happy is the bride that the sun shines on.* I remember feeling very nervous as we walked into the church where the organ was playing Grieg's wedding march. When I met Eric at the altar he just pressed my little finger and I felt reassured and my nervousness disappeared. I enjoyed the service immensely. It is an unforgettable experience. We left the church to the strains of *Greensleeves* on the organ. I had gone into the church on the arm of my brother, who gave me away, and, now that it was all over, I had the arm of my husband. I was quite a while getting used to the word 'husband'. In fact for some time after my marriage I still signed my maiden name. Perhaps many brides do.

Coming out of the church we were overwhelmed with photographers and little children giving me wooden spoons trimmed with bows of ribbon. I think I collected no less than five of them, as well as numerous horseshoes. The church bells too helped to make it a festive occasion.

Back we went to my mother's house for the small reception. Although our house was small everybody was well catered for. As we were going off that evening to Brighton for our honeymoon someone had arranged to take us by car to Peterborough to catch the London train at six o'clock.

At last we could relax knowing it was all over and everything had turned out as planned. We changed at King's Cross for Victoria and the Brighton train and arrived at about nine-thirty. A taxi took us to the Neville House Hotel. By this time I was quite hungry as I hadn't eaten much all day. A cold meal was waiting for us in the dining room of the hotel. We did it justice too. By the time supper was finished it was creeping on towards eleven o'clock.

Our room was on the first floor. It all seemed very luxurious. There was a phone in the room and 'all mod. cons.' I pulled out a dress from the suitcase and was about to hang it in the wardrobe when Eric told me to stop. Confetti was everywhere. Someone had managed to get into the case, which had been locked, and sprinkled confetti all over the clothes. Before leaving my mother's house we had brushed off any confetti which had caught us and it was combed out of my hair. We thought that was the end of it all. Eric wasn't amused and thought it a very poor joke.

I enjoyed every moment of that week at Brighton. It was very pleasant for walking. The sunshine and the sea breeze were just the thing to give one a good appetite. I looked forward to each meal. I even enjoyed a cooked breakfast, which I never had at home.

We spent our evenings in the hotel lounge which we usually had to ourselves. I suppose it was a little too early in the year for the visitors. Eric had unearthed a book in the hotel library which he wanted to read to me. This was *Madame Curie*. We managed to get through it before the end of the week. That was the start of the many books he read to me.

Our week's holiday went by all too quickly. It was back to work on the following Monday. Our bedsitter was rather cramped but we knew it was only a temporary measure for we had the promise of two flats - one with the LCC and one at Hackney. The latter was privately owned. Eric had to be up very early in the morning to get a train to Hayes in Middlesex to start work at eight whereas I didn't have to be at work till nine. He made his own breakfast of porridge and toast. He left my porridge in the double saucepan to keep warm. I am afraid there were one or two mornings when I dropped off to sleep again after he had left and had no time for breakfast. In order to be sure of being at work by nine I had to be in the bus queue by eight-thirty. Sometimes there was quite a long queue, especially on a wet day when those going short distances also took the bus instead of walking to work. I had previously had sandwiches for lunch and my evening meal at the hostel. Now I had a proper lunch, sometimes in our canteen in Whitehall or sometimes going out with a friend. Then in the evening we had a light meal. The small cooking ring in one corner of our bedsitter was rather difficult for a blind person to negotiate. Eric was quite adept at managing it. It was surprising what one could do on a small ring. He could even cook a small pot roast. He excelled at making omelets. He would say: "When we get our flat and a cooker you can take over and cook everything." I was just longing to try out all the recipes I had been taught at my cookery lessons.

In spite of all the limitations in this one room, we were happy. I wished it to last for a very long time. Eric sometimes remarked that this was too good to last and something was sure to come to end it all. I couldn't see why just then. I have often thought about his words since.

I looked forward to our walks in Kensington Gardens in the evening. We watched some ducks each night on the Round Pond. They were only tiny chicks when we were first married. As the weeks passed by we could see them growing bigger. When the evenings became warmer we found a seat in a quiet spot and he would read to me. We knew that when we got our flat there would be chores to do in the evenings and the weekends. We didn't have to clean our room as it was serviced by the landlady. She didn't like us even to make our own beds. She supplied all the linen. We only had our washing-up to do after meals. The room was always spotless. One was almost afraid of spoiling the nice carpet. However, we were together and knew suitable accommodation would come along eventually. This would meet all our needs for a year or so when we intended buying a house of our own. We had already consulted building societies and had started to save for a mortgage. In fact we made many plans.

This summer of 1952 was lived to the full. We attended several Promenade concerts. The Royal Albert Hall was only minutes away. Sometimes we walked there through Kensington Gardens. These concerts gave me a much better understanding of good music. Apart from work, there was always something to look forward to. We often visited Richmond at weekends and took afternoon tea in the restaurant in Richmond Park.

At the end of July we decided to take a fortnight's holiday at Eastbourne. This was most enjoyable. The sun shone all the way. I remember the concerts in the bandstand in the afternoons and theatres in the evening. The hotel dinners were first class. In fact so were all the meals. We had a large breakfast rather late and cut out lunch. We did such a lot and saw so much in that two weeks of holiday that I wondered if it had been a lovely dream.

Our holiday over and back in London we settled down to the daily routine. We looked forward to the weekends. Eric did the weekly shopping on Saturday mornings while I was at work. Certain foods were still on ration. I remember that we were allowed two eggs, a quarter of a pound of tea, and a pound of sugar between us to last the week. When all the shopping was done and the laundry sorted out he took a bus to Whitehall to meet me from the office and take me out for lunch. Some Saturday afternoons we went shopping in the Edgware Road market. I remember things were supposed to be cheaper there. We tried to buy something each week towards our home.

On Saturday 15th September we received notice of a flat to let at Hackney and as we were fairly high on the housing list they asked us if we were still interested. That Saturday afternoon we decided to go and look at it. We found it needed quite a lot of decorating. Eric decided that, after the necessary painting and papering, it would suit us for a temporary period. Subject to confirmation by the Housing Committee, which was meeting the following week, the flat was ours. On the way back we looked at one or two furniture shop windows. In our wanderings we came across a very nice furniture shop near Whiteley's in Queensway. There was just the bedroom suite we wanted and had the shop not been closed on Saturday afternoon we would most certainly have placed a deposit on it.

A week later on Sunday 23rd September Eric was unwell. He thought it was indigestion and tried various remedies. He carried on with the usual preparations for lunch. He didn't seem to improve. He prepared lunch for me but wasn't having any himself. We ended up with neither of us having anything to eat. In the afternoon we decided to go and find a doctor. We tried at least three doctors. All were either off duty or away on holiday. This was getting us nowhere. All the time the pain in his chest was becoming worse. I had a brainwave. I thought that if we went to the casualty department of St. Mary's Hospital they were bound to look at him. We took a bus to the hospital in Paddington where the doctor on duty saw Eric immediately. After a brief examination we were told that he would have to go into hospital for a few days under observation. He had been given an injection and the pain was much relieved. However, they decided to move him to the hospital in Harrow Road. The ambulance would take us to the hospital and when he had been settled in would take me home. I sat and waited a few minutes when the ambulance driver told me that they had to return to their station in case they were required for an emergency and must take me back straight away.

I was taken to see Eric who was being examined by more doctors. He spoke to me reassuringly and said he would be alright. The ambulance staff saw me back as instructed. By this time it was late Sunday evening. I climbed the four flights of stairs, unlocked the door of our room, and on entering turned the key in the lock again. This is where I went to rock bottom. I felt something must be very wrong with Eric. I tried my best to believe he would soon be with me again. I did not sleep and cried nonstop all night. I heard a church clock strike every quarter of an hour. The house was very quiet, as it usually was. We seldom heard a sound from the other tenants.

About seven o'clock in the morning I could hear the front door bell ringing. I felt sure it was bad news. About twenty minutes later there was a tap on my door. It was the warden of the hostel. The couple who owned the house could not both be away at any one time. One of them must remain in charge. When the message came from the hospital that Eric had passed away it was such a shock to the landlord as he did not even know that Eric had been taken ill. He couldn't break the news to me but phoned the warden of the hostel to ask her to do so.

I did not need telling. Something or someone told me. The warden came over to my bed and said: "You will have to be a brave girl when I tell you that Eric has died in the early hours." She stayed with me and saw to my breakfast which I couldn't touch.

She had been asked to take me to the hospital as the doctor wished to speak to me. As we were walking along the street on the way to Harrow Road Hospital one of the slabs on the pavement gave way as I was walking over it. I slipped into the hole and had the warden not been holding me I would have fallen into a cellar. Apparently the coalman had not replaced the slab properly after delivering coal. To add to my misery both my legs were skinned and my stockings ripped to shreds. I was in a real mess. Before we could see the doctor we spent half the morning in the casualty ward having my legs cleaned up and bandaged.

We eventually saw the doctor who had attended Eric. He just wanted to offer condolences and to say that Eric had not suffered in any way. This was not much comfort in my state of mind.

The warden was a real friend. She did all the arranging. Without her help I shouldn't have had the slightest idea how to go about things. In the course of the morning it suddenly dawned on me that I must let the office know why I had not turned up for work that day. I phoned from the house. An hour or so later my supervisor came to me in my bedsitter and told me she was coming to stay with me each night until the funeral. She also told me that there had been a phone call that morning telling me we had been allocated the flat we had viewed the previous week. I had to turn it down. I would not have been able to cope. In any case I could not have afforded to pay for all the cleaning and decorating.

The funeral took place the following Thursday at Paddington cemetery which was right out at Mill Hill East. Several of my family and office friends attended. I had been granted compassionate leave from work.

After the funeral I went home to my mother for a week. I then returned to London as the doctor thought I would feel better with something to occupy my mind. I found that to be quite true. The ordeal had certainly given me a shaking. It was two years before I could take any real interest in anything.

10.

LONDON - ALONE AGAIN

After spending just over a week with my mother I returned to work. My morale couldn't have been lower. All my hopes· and plans had been shattered. One day everything had looked good. Then all at once the bottom had dropped out of my world. I realised, of course, that I would have to pull myself together again. That wasn't as easy as perhaps it sounds. My legs were still bad from the accident. Being at home meant I could not attend hospital. The local district nurse visited me and dressed them a few times, one leg having become infected. I am glad to say that they eventually healed up quite well and gave me no further trouble.

It must have been the beginning of October when I returned to London. My landlady greeted me on arrival and did all she could to help me, telling me to knock on her door if I should be in any difficulty. The autumn of 1952 was a very wet one. It had simply poured down with rain ever since Eric had died. My doctor was right; I did feel better working. My colleagues were marvellous and I couldn't have had kinder folk around me. When I returned in the evenings to my bedsitter my landlady had drawn the curtains and lit the small gas fire. I would find either her dog, Hamish, or her cat, Vicky, sitting on my rug and greeting me as I entered. I was most appreciative of this kind thought for one can feel very lonely in a bedsitter.

With the meagre facilities in my room my evening meal would consist of sandwiches or something on toast. The gas ring was too near the curtains and I felt it very risky to use the frying pan. I could get cooked ham, bread, cakes, etc. from the Express Dairy in Whitehall and I could manage as I always had a good lunch. After my meal in the evening I settled down to read or listen to the radio. During the evening my landlady would often come up to see if everything was all right. She was concerned, I think, whether I was eating properly. However, she didn't have to worry too much about the weekends as I was away for many of them. I went home to my mother every third weekend and stayed with friends for the others. This period of my life was about the dullest I had known. Even the weather was as grim as it could be. It rained, so it seems to me on looking back, almost every day.

In early November London was in the grip of a terrible fog (smog). It lasted six days. Going out in the morning to get the bus to work was dreadful. Although I wore a thick scarf over my mouth I could still taste the smokey fog. It made me cough and hurt my throat. The fog never lifted. I was glad that the bus stop was only five minutes away from the digs. The smell of the fog permeated through the house and I couldn't open my bedroom window. On the Saturday I went to visit my friends at Eastcote, Middlesex. They met me when I left work at 12.30. When we got to Eastcote station there were no taxis so we had to walk about a mile to their house. It was a bit easier to breathe there. How grateful I was to be in a warm house sitting in front of a real fire instead of my little gas fire! During the weekend the fog began to lift and a fine drizzle set in. Though it was damp and cold anything was better than the fog.

It was back to London on Monday morning for work at nine. I am sure that work was my salvation at this time. During the day I hadn't much time to think of myself and had people to talk to. There was no future to look forward to and in the evenings sitting over my gas fire I would try to recapture the happy memories of the past summer.

Near the end of November I was just about to catch my bus for work when there was a knock on my door. As I unlocked the door I heard the voice of the warden of the hostel. She had come to tell me that my old room at the hostel had become vacant and that if I wished I could return. I was pleased to accept and I knew that my landlady would be too. I had been away from the hostel for only eight months. What a lot had happened in that short space of time.

The following day was Saturday. During the afternoon some of my friends helped me to move my few belongings back to my old room, which I was to share with the same girl. At least there would be a good meal to look forward to in the evening. Food was proving to be a problem as some things were still on ration and by Saturday afternoon there wasn't much left in the shops.

1953 wasn't a very eventful year. There was the Coronation of course. The hostel residents were invited to attend the ceremony in Westminster Abbey. I did not go but those who did had to be in their seats behind the organ by seven a.m. Those who were lucky enough to get window seats in Whitehall also had to be in their places very early as the streets were closed for reasons of security. I preferred to stay in the hostel and listen to the service on the radio. It rained most of the day. I remember leaving the office on the day before the Coronation and finding the pavement outside crowded with people intending to have a good view the following day. They were camping on the pavements all along Whitehall and up to Westminster tube station. One of the girls from my office guided me through the crowds to my bus stop. I was glad that the next day was a holiday.

It must have been at least two years before I began to take an interest in evening classes again and enrolled at the City Literary Institute, this time deciding on Shakespeare. I also rejoined the London Sports Club for the Blind. I still missed all the good times at weekends, such as a meal out on Friday evenings and the theatre visit on Saturdays. That summer I had attended two Promenade concerts on my own and a piano recital in the Queen Elizabeth Hall.

In 1956 the Civil Service at last got the five-day week. I was glad for I could now go home on Friday evening and return on Sunday evening without having to take annual leave. We also received a pay increase that year. I was pleased to be given a room of my own in the hostel. The previous occupier had managed to secure a flat near her place of work.

In 1957 I decided that I would like to have my own flat. I set about this by visiting the blind welfare department at County Hall during the lunch hour. The home teacher for the blind filled up the necessary application forms for me and I was included on the LCC waiting list. When I told my mother about this she did not think much of it. She made her usual remark that I would never manage on my own. However, I just pressed ahead and hoped it wouldn't be too long before my wish came true. I realised it would be more expensive than living in the hostel. Having lived most of my life in school, college, hostels, and with my parents, I had suddenly got the urge to have a home of my own. I decided one didn't have to be married to do that. Anyway I hadn't the slightest intention of marrying again.

In the spring of 1958 the LCC housing department wrote to say that an officer wished to interview me. I took a day's annual leave and waited in my room until the Housing Inspector arrived in the early afternoon. He only stayed about five minutes and asked me a few questions. He was interviewing people for some new flats nearing completion in Lancaster Gate. It would be just right for me as it was on my bus route for work. I wondered how long I would have to wait. I was looking forward to choosing the furniture for which Eric and I had saved.

About three months later, in early July, I heard that I had been allocated a single flat in Carroll House, Lancaster Gate. The rent would be £12 a month and the rates £36 each half year. £72 in a full year for rates was rather staggering. Still I had recently received a pay rise and I felt I could manage. I got a friend to take me to the flats to find out which one I was to have. A few were already occupied. I was shown a flat on the second floor and the one immediately above it on the third floor. I was advised to take the one on the third floor as it would be less noisy being that little bit higher above street level. I paid the caretaker to fix curtain rails and wash out the place. It was all very exciting. A friend went with me on Saturday morning to buy a gas cooker, an Ideal Homes one with two rings and a grill above the oven. It would be fixed the following week. The caretaker would attend to everything. That Saturday evening I had booked to go to a Promenade concert. One of the pieces of music I had been looking forward to hearing was Beethoven's Symphony No. 3 (the Eroica). Try as I might to concentrate on this, one of my favourites, the thought of my new gas cooker would creep into my mind. Whenever I hear the Eroica I think of that first gas cooker.

The next important item was the curtains. One lunch hour a friend from work went to my flat and measured up for curtains and carpets. I could only afford a carpet for the lounge-cum-bedroom. The rest of the flat had polished tiles which meant plenty of hard work in polishing. I had to wait until late August before Selfridges had made the curtains and I was able to move in.

The day came at last. I moved into my own home, just a

single flat with lounge and bedroom combined. The divan bed was at one end but with the tapestry cover and cushions to match the curtains it wasn't so obvious as a bed and people told me the colour scheme was just right. I had learnt how to use the new gas cooker and I was anxious to experiment with cooking. The kitchenette was very well appointed. I spent many happy hours working in it. It was good to be able to entertain my friends for a change. Hitherto it had always been the reverse. The only thing I could complain about was that the noise from the traffic kept me awake at night. It must be one of the noisiest areas in London. There was a Chinese restaurant next to the flats, a night club quite close, and a taxi rank opposite which operated at all hours. To get a tiny bit of peace one had to close the windows which was stifling in hot weather. Nevertheless one does become immune to extraneous noises – eventually!

In those days there was no mobility training for the blind and I remember spending a whole Sunday morning learning my way about the area. Lancaster Gate station was only a few minutes walk along the Bayswater Road as was the bus stop I needed for work. The return journey wasn't quite so simple, as the bus stopped on the other side of the Bayswater Road and I had to get help to cross. I found no difficulty in this whatever time in the evening I returned.

Sometimes on Sunday mornings I would take myself for a walk along the Bayswater Road on the park side. It was a good wide pavement with no crossings right up to Marble Arch. I turned back there for the pavement was cluttered with pavement artists and crowds of people. In the summer months I had the Sports Club rambles. As I had a weight problem I took every opportunity of a walk during the winter though it wasn't much fun walking alone. This is something I dare not have done in my home town. I never went out alone in Spalding where I was fairly well known and where I felt people would be looking at me. In London I stopped at nothing. My white stick was my lucky charm. People seeing this would always come to the rescue.

In January 1961 my mother died after a short illness. The house in Spalding was given up. I would miss the weekends spent at home. By this time all my brothers and sisters were married and in homes of their own. There would be no occasion for me to make further visits to Spalding.

1963 was a very long winter with lots of snow. Although the roads and streets were very treacherous, I managed not to lose a day's work. I remember wearing men's socks over my boots. Friends kept me supplied with worn-out socks and I am glad to say I never slipped on the ice. One of my blind friends did sustain a bad fracture and was off work a long time.

That spring I joined the tandem section of the Blind Sports Club. A sighted front rider was found for me and we cycled sometimes several miles on Sunday mornings. It was a very pleasant experience although the weather was cold. During this year also I was successful in passing my shorthand examination for 120 w.p.m. Now I had managed to secure the proficiency allowance in both shorthand and typing. It had taken a long time but I did get there in the end. In August a blind friend and I went to Guernsey for a fortnight's holiday on our own. She told me that she dare do the journey if I dare. I wondered how we would manage as neither of us had any sight at all. We decided to go by boat as it was quite a lot cheaper than flying. I wrote to the blind welfare in Guernsey to ask if one of their staff would show us the way round St. Peter Port on the first day.

The day for our holiday arrived. My friend, Barbara, met me at Paddington where we took the train to Victoria. A kindly porter saw us on to the Weymouth train. We couldn't afford to take taxis in those days so we were both fairly cluttered, carrying suitcase, handbag, and white stick. At Weymouth we were soon helped on to the boat. We were treated like VIP's. It was about lunch time and we were both given free tickets for lunch. We were escorted into the restaurant and taken to a table. The staff had taken care of our luggage. After lunch we were advised not to sit on deck as it was too windy. We were put into the first-class lounge although neither of us had a first-class ticket. We were very comfortable there though I was disappointed at not being able to sit on deck and enjoy the sea air.

We arrived at St. Peter Port in the late afternoon and were met by the hotel taxi which had been laid on for us. This was the farthest either of us had ever travelled. The hotel mangeress showed us our room and our table in the dining-room. This was Saturday and if anyone had intended to come and help us from the blind welfare we knew it wouldn't be before Monday. After dinner we decided to spend the evening in our room. It all seemed rather strange at first.

On the following morning we enquired how far it was to the nearest church. The person who directed us made it sound very easy. Our hotel was in Queen's Road which was a very quiet road at that time. We simply turned right out of this road and followed the sound of the bells to church. We spoke to a couple of people who guided us into the church, St. James the Less. At the end of the service a couple came up to us and asked if they could be of any help. That was the start of our good luck. We told them we were new to the island and wanted to learn our way around. They lived in Belmont Road, the next road along from our hotel.

That afternoon they took us out to show us the lie of the land. They showed us how to get into the town and explained where the shops and harbour were. There were seats where we would later sit. It was thanks to these people that we, managed to find our way around long before the end of the fortnight. It was a good thing we had met someone to show us the layout for the blind welfare never materialised. The weather was just glorious sunshine all the way. We were taken round the little chapel built by the monks, the whole of the interior walls of which were covered with broken china, beautifully patterned and blended together. We were also taken to see the famous glasshouses. We could not touch the flowers of course but one of the workmen described them to us. The perfume from some of them was glorious. A couple of days later there was a bowl of roses on our table at the hotel. The owners of the glasshouses had sent them for us.

The fortnight seemed to pass in no time. We intended to go again. We had made some good friends. The couple we met at church invited us round to tea several times and we kept up a correspondence with them for years. We came away from Guernsey with the full allowance of our favourite perfume but not with our drink or cigarette allowance. A day or two later we received a large box of Guernsey tomatoes from some kind person. We never found out from whom. I shall never forget that holiday. I still count it as one of the best.

In 1964 I decided to apply for a change of accommodation to a lower rated zone. The rents and rates for the Lancaster Gate flats were increasing all the time. During my lunch hour one day

I took myself up to the Housing Department at County Hall and stated my case. I was told they would do what they could. They were true to their word for very soon after that they offered me a similar flat in Ruskin Park House, near to Denmark Hill station. The bus stop was just at the top of the road. The bus fare was just the same as previously, although I now had to change buses at Camberwell Green. As my rent and rates were now halved I was quite well off in comparison.

During my first week in my new flat I was fortunate enough to have a small boy to escort me to my bus. After that I was quite familiar with the route. Ruskin Park House was well away from the road in its own grounds and therefore much quieter at nights. My flat was on the second floor. The lounge was large with a balcony and windows which looked out on to the gardens of the estate which were kept very nicely. The kitchenette was just about the size of my previous one with plenty of cupboard space and walls tiled to halfway. The bathroom was the largest I had seen and tiled all over. The only sad feature was that I was debarred from attending evening classes as I was nervous of walking from the bus late at night. It was so quiet after ten in the evening. I didn't mind it earlier in the evenings when other people were leaving work.

My friends visited me at weekends. There were window boxes the length of the balcony and I took an interest in growing small flowers. One year I grew some stocks and when the door to the balcony was open their fragrant perfume permeated the whole flat. My journey from work in the evenings was much quicker for I missed the traffic jams in Oxford Street.

These last few years of my working life were happy and contented ones. I was enjoying my work and all my friends. I was also quite happy in my flat. The time would soon come when I must make up my mind about the future. I knew I must decide whether to spend my retirement in London or to return to my own area where the cost of living would be lower.

Eric - when we first met

Mr. & Mrs. Eric Wheel 15th March 1952

Mr. & Mrs. Ernest Clarke 3rd April 1972

Mobility training in Boston.
Alan Wedgbury, Mobility Officer for the blind for Lincolnshire,
my training officer in the background

11.

SOUTH-EAST LONDON AND CROWLAND

Having settled down in my new accommodation in South East London, and become familiar with the layout of my new surroundings, I realised all the advantages of the change. Apart from the quicker journey I could now do my shopping on the way home from work. On Fridays I broke my journey at East Lane market where I could get most things. There were cut-price shops and a very good Marks and Spencer where the food section was excellent. The staff there were most helpful and used to look out for me with my white stick. This stick was a real asset for, no matter how busy the staff were, someone came to my rescue immediately.

There was a very frequent bus service even on Sundays. I could get a bus direct from Ruskin Park to King's Cross Station. This was very convenient when I visited my family in Crowland. I would go to Peterborough where one of the family always met me. Someone would take me to Peterborough to see me on to the King's Cross train for the return journey. It was a cold journey in winter and that was probably one of the things which helped me to decide that, when the time came, I would try to return to my home area.

The time arrived when I had to think seriously about my retirement. I turned the matter over in my mind quite a lot and discussed it with friends and colleagues, some of whom would be retiring out of London. Early in 1967 I wrote to the Rural District Council in my home area. I enquired about accommodation in Crowland, near to my family, and asked whether the fact that I had been living out of the area for twenty years would affect my chances of returning. At the same time I wrote to three people on the local council asking for help. Two of the three replied that they would do what they could. After a brief period I heard from the District Council that they were in the course of erecting a block of flats in Crowland for retired people and that my name had been included on the waiting list of prospective tenants.

About six months before my sixtieth birthday I received a letter from the Establishments Division saying that if I wished to do so I could carry on working until the age of sixty-five when my position would be reviewed in the light of my performance at that time. After consideration I felt I should retire as there was the likelihood of accommodation when the Crowland flats for retired people were completed. I simply dare not turn down the council's offer as I might never get another chance of moving back to my home area. In fact I worked another eighteen months after the age of sixty. I still enjoyed my work. The fact that I had accomplished what I had set out to do gave me some consolation for all the hard work in the early days. I should have liked to have done better. This might have been possible had I started at a younger age. I was also proud of having been a blood donor for nearly twenty years and felt that I had been of some use to the community.

About six weeks before I retired I spent a long weekend with my sister in Crowland. During the time I was there she took me to see the new flats which were nearing completion. Although I knew I had been allocated a flat I did not know which one it was likely to be. The workmen showed us one of the flats on the ground floor. While I liked the layout and the fact that the flats were in their own grounds and away from the road, there were one or two small features I didn't like. There was no private letter-box in the front door but an individual pigeon hole in the front hall. Also there was only one bathroom between every four tenants. I tried not to let this bother me too much. For several years I had had my own letter-box and bathroom in my flat.

When I returned to work one of my bosses asked me what I thought of the new abode. I mentioned these two disadvantages. He asked me if I wished to reverse my decision to retire. I didn't think so.

When the Crowland flats were completed I was notified that I had been allocated a single flat on the ground floor. Then I decided on the date of my retirement. I hoped that I was doing the right thing. I felt that if I let this opportunity pass me by I would probably be stuck in London for the rest of my life. The time might come when I could not get around so easily. I might then have regrets.

I intended to stay active and had plenty of ideas of how I would spend my new leisure.

The date of my retirement arrived. All the work I did that morning was to type three short minutes and sign the Official Secrets Act which all Civil Servants are required to do. In the afternoon the office gave me a farewell party. I received gifts from all the young girls in the typing pool, the supervisor, and a cheque from the people for whom I worked. I bought a new vacuum cleaner with this. Someone had taken the trouble to have all the names of all the people who had contributed brailled on the retirement card. It took up several pages. I shall always remember that last evening when I stepped on to the No.12 bus clutching an armful of flowers. That was perhaps one of my most emotional experiences.

The following week I spent packing up and clearing my London flat. I had arranged for a London firm to move my belongings to Crowland. They arrived about 8.00 a.m. and whilst they were packing up my home I travelled by train to Peterborough where my sister was to meet me. I left everything to the removal men who handed in the keys of the flat to the caretaker as they left.

This was not the last time I did that journey. I very often travelled up to London after I retired to shop in the West End or visit my friend in Lancaster Gate.

On the removal day I was in Crowland having coffee with my sister by eleven o'clock.

There I was now living in Crowland. I was pleased with the new flat and with the way my furniture and belongings had fitted in. I quite enjoyed not having to get up at six-thirty in the morning and wait at the bus stop in all weathers to get to work.

The first thing I had to do was to learn my way around. I had help from my two sisters who lived in different parts of the town. When I had been shown a few times I managed to find their houses without help. I went astray only once but I don't think anyone saw me. On my way to have lunch with one of them I had to cross a patch of grass which led to a path. This I did quite satisfactorily. However, along the road there was a house in the course of construction. This is where I went wrong. I veered too much to one side and dropped into quite a deep hole full of builder's sand. I just dug my white stick into the ground outside the hole and climbed out, found the grass verge again, and proceeded on my way. I wasn't in any way hurt but my shoes and coat were in rather a mess.

Another time, on one of my shopping expeditions, I entered what I was quite sure was the grocers. I couldn't hear or smell anything as I suffered from hay fever for months after I retired. I heard a man's voice say: "Do you want a short back and sides?" I realised then where I was. Very soon I managed to find the shops without any difficulty and in fact I even took myself for short walks round the flats.

That same summer I decided to arrange a fortnight's holiday at the Blind Holiday Home in Hunstanton to see if the sea air would clear up my hay fever. By then I had got a telephone installed in my flat and was able to make the necessary arrangements very quickly. The holiday was fixed and I was on my way. I remember having to change buses at least three times. A taxi was waiting for me at Hunstanton and I arrived on the doorstep hungry and all hot and bothered. I think I was invited to sit down and then came the warden who said: "Can you see at all?" When I told him that I couldn't he said: "We like all blind people to have a guide". I thought what a greeting after the hazardous journey. I told him I was very independent and wouldn't bother the staff very much. I believe he was new to the job and had no experience of blind people. When he found I needed very little assistance he was quite helpful. I could understand his concern when I met some of the other guests who were elderly and frail both physically and mentally.

I had a very nice single room and the food was good. The home was situated not far from the sea and there were gardens quite near with plenty of seats on which to sit and enjoy the summer weather. At first I didn't get very far afield on my own but this didn't bother me for I had my knitting, reading, and pocket radio. I had been there only a few days when I met two ladies who took me under their wing. They met me every day and took me around with them. We went for walks, for morning coffee, and to concerts. I enjoyed the fortnight and am glad to say that my hay-fever disappeared and I have had no trouble since.

In the autumn I applied to the Ministry of Labour in Peterborough for a part-time shorthand and typing job as I seemed to have so much time on my hands. I felt a part-time job might help me adjust to retirement. Within a few days my telephone rang one morning asking me to attend for interview at a garage in Peterborough. I got my sister to go with me so that I could judge whether I could manage the journey. I decided I would like to work three days a week. At that time I could earn £30 a month without losing any of my pension. I got the job.

This small office was above a garage. There was a small staff of four including the secretary. The telephonist who lived in Crowland was willing to accompany me from the bus to the office and vice versa. If she had to work late I could make my own way to the bus stop. The girls in the office were all very young and I found them very friendly and helpful. My very small room had only a tiny electric fire for heating. It was September and quite pleasant walking from the bus stop along the Lincoln Road. I didn't have much work to do. The very short letters I had to type, many of them repetitive and boring, were very different from my work in the Civil Service. Most of the words were unfamiliar for I knew very little about cars and their components. I certainly wasn't occupied to the limit of my capacity. Some days I received no work until late afternoon. As I worked only every other day this meant I must complete that day's work before I left the office. It was a very pleasant autumn and the warm sun streamed through my window. While waiting for work I occupied my time by reading and typing my own private letters. I also typed my Christmas cards and letters early, something I had never had time for previously.

However as the weeks went by the weather grew colder and I was glad of the small electric fire. I remember one very foggy night in early December the little girl from Crowland and I had difficulty in finding the bus stop. It was a freezing fog and the cold seemed to get into one's bones. We learned that the buses had stopped because of the fog. There was nothing else we could do but return to the garage and see what could be done to get us home. A young couple offered to take us home in their car. There never was a time when I was more grateful for help. This couple were going out of their way as they lived in the opposite direction. The fog wasn't quite so dense outside the city. None of us were any the worse for the experience. How I appreciated my centrally-heated flat that night!

We were now within a few days of Christmas. I had been working for nearly four months. I still did not get sufficient work to keep me going all the time but I was ticking over nicely just working every other day. I was preparing for Christmas in Crowland. I remember setting up a Christmas tree decorated with coloured lights. I knew that I would not be able to see the effect but my nieces seemed to enjoy it. The carol singers entertained us in the evenings.

On the last working day before Christmas I arrived at the office to find a turkey with all its feathers lying on the floor of my room. It was a Christmas present from the firm. Everyone working in the garage received one. Mine weighed eleven pounds. I was rather shattered at the size for I knew it was much too large for me. Mine was the least heavy for some weighed twenty pounds. I decided it had better go to my sister where I would be spending Christmas as she had a family to feed. I couldn't touch it as it lay there and kept well away from it as I moved about the room. This was the first time I had received a Christmas gift from my employers. I thought at the time I would have preferred a box of chocolates. I was sitting at my desk wondering how I could get this bird to Crowland on the bus. A young man from the firm offered to take it to my sister's house and needless to say they were surprised and delighted. My brother-in-law dressed it and prepared it for the table.

This Christmas was a particularly enjoyable one as I had my own home and could entertain the family in my flat. On Christmas Eve a friend and I attended the midnight service in Crowland Abbey. This was quite an exciting experience. I remember we walked back to the flats round about one-thirty and had sherry and mince pies. About mid-morning on Christmas Day I walked to my sister's house where I stayed until Boxing Day. Then I entertained various members of the family in my flat.

New Year's Eve was quite jolly too for there was a party in the community centre at the flats. We had a meal and entertainment during the evening ending at midnight with the singing of Auld Lang Syne.

The following Monday I returned to the office. The weather was becoming colder. We had snow which froze hard on the pavements and I had thoughts of giving up the job. I had not forgotten the appalling weather of 1963 when I never missed a day's work although the snow was piled up on the roads. This wasn't as bad as that. I think the breaking point really came when I arrived in the office on a very cold morning and my small fire was giving out very little heat. I could hardly feel my typewriter keys. The very last straw was when I was told that there was a mouse in my waste-paper basket. On reflection I remember hearing strange noises when all was quiet. I decided to resign and left at the end of January. Since the weather became worse after that I never regretted the move. I did not try for any further part-time jobs but sometimes did some private work.

I can remember that spring with its power cuts at various times of the day. I spent many days with my sisters both of whom had coal fires so their heating wasn't affected. I made sure I walked somewhere every day. I scarcely ever sat down doing nothing. Quite often I went to London to shop at Marks and Spencers at Marble Arch or to spend a weekend with my friend.

The summer of 1970 was quite a happy one for me. I was enjoying my leisure and getting out and about quite a bit. I joined the Blind Sunshine Club in Peterborough which met on alternate Friday afternoons. They usually had a speaker or someone to entertain us. It was quite a large gathering including half-a-dozen guide dogs. There were outings to various places and a big dinner at Christmas. Some Sunday evenings I would take myself to Peterborough to listen to the Salvation Army band which at that time was one of the best in the country. They certainly did have some very talented players and the music was superb. After the evening service someone would always see me on to my bus. On Sunday mornings I attended the service in Crowland Abbey.

In the spring the warden and her friends had decorated the flat for me. Although the flats had only been built two years the decoration was pretty shabby and most of the tenants were redecorating. The ladies certainly made my flat look nice. I was most grateful and pleased as I have always been very houseproud – and still am. I had fulfilled a very longstanding ambition. I had for a long time wanted red velvet curtains. Now I had managed to get them at last. The large window showed them off very well. I had been a great collector of records and tapes. Most of my old records were mono though my latest ones were stereo. At that time I did a lot of my correspondence with my old friends on tape. I liked to hear their news though I sometimes found my own rather sparse for each day was very much like the last. I was also a member of two tape clubs.

That Christmas was also a memorable one as one of my nieces was married on Boxing Day at Gedney parish church. I attended with my sister. This was a very jolly way to round off the Christmas festivities.

12.

ERNIE, BOSTON, AND THE PATCHWORK QUILT

The early weeks of 1971 were rather wintry with nothing very exciting to report. The evenings seemed endless. I managed to occupy myself during the day, given fine weather, when I could walk round to my sisters' or do my shopping. I made a point of visiting London about once a month, sometimes staying with a friend for the weekend. I felt sure that I had done the right thing by retiring to the country. My two pensions might not have stretched to meet the cost of living had I remained in London whereas in Crowland I found my income fairly adequate.

This was when I got the idea of writing a book to fill up the long evenings. It was difficult at first to know where to start. Years ago a friend had suggested I write my story as I had led quite a varied existence starting in a remote cottage in the wilds of Lincolnshire and then on to Whitehall. With nothing better to do I started to type the account of my early life. This did help the evenings along. The only drawback was that, as I was unable to see what I had written, I quite often spent a whole evening typing only to tear it all up and drop it into the waste-paper basket. Then I decided to braille it first so that I could see what it looked like before I typed it. This was a more tidy way of doing things though it was time consuming, but time was what I had plenty of just then. At least it did keep me awake and alert. I found listening to the radio sometimes sent me to sleep.

In May I was told of a craft class in Boston on Wednesdays and I was invited to join as I was always anxious to learn fresh crafts. So each Wednesday I travelled from Crowland to Boston, changing buses at Spalding. Not only did I learn how to make plant pot holders and cuddly toys but I also met fresh people. I believe the age range was from the twenties to over sixty.

In July I was invited to join the blind social club in Boston which had recently been set up. They held their meeting once a month at Sunniholme in Tower Road. The blind home that I had lived in in Pen Street before the war had moved to this much more spacious house with its large garden early in the 1960s. The old house in Pen Street had become a dental surgery. At the August meeting I was asked to sit on their committee as one of their number had died and I held this position for about twelve years. I resigned in February 1985 mainly because I had joined a literary class at Pilgrim College which was held on the same morning as our social club meetings. I also felt it was time I gave someone else a chance to serve.

Now back to the August 1971 meeting where I met the other members of the committee. After the meeting one of the members, a gentleman named Ernie, offered to escort me to the dining room for lunch. He showed me to my place at the table and disappeared to his own table. After lunch he came back and asked me if I would like to walk round the garden with some of the other people. He guided me round and showed me the layout. What struck me about this garden was the guiding-rope round the pathways to help blind folk find their way independently. This impressed me as I am myself rather bothered by open spaces.

After our walk Ernie showed me to my place in the craft room. That was all I saw of him that day as I was given a lift by car to the bus stop and never gave him any further thought. The following week I attended the craft class as usual. During the morning the teacher was trying to organise an outing for the following Wednesday. Ernie, who was partially sighted, offered to act as my guide. The outing was to Woodhall Spa with tea at the 'Cafe in the Woods'. The day of the outing was a beautiful one in early September. When we arrived at Woodhall we were told we could go our own ways and meet at the cafe at four-thirty where tea had been arranged. The walk through the woods was very pleasant on this glorious day. An excellent tea was provided and everyone enjoyed the afternoon out. We were back in Boston by six o'clock in time for me to catch my bus home. I saw no more of Ernie for a fortnight.

Early one Sunday morning about the end of September the telephone rang: my sister in Boston asked me over for tea and said they would meet me off the bus. When I arrived at her house there was Ernie who had also been invited. I wondered if this was just coincidental. Anyway it was a surprise. After tea Ernie suggested we attend the evening service at the Hospital Bridge Church. He would see me on to my bus afterwards. It was obvious he was well known at this church where he introduced me to his friends and to the Minister, the Reverend Herrick. When the service was over he invited us both to the Manse for coffee. He saw me on to my bus and then drove Ernie home.

It had been a very pleasant evening and I had met new people many of whom were later to become friends. I had to change buses at Spalding where there was an hour's wait for the Crowland bus. I didn't like that long wait on a more or less deserted coach station. I found the place rather cold and spooky. I decided I wouldn't do this very often particularly during the winter months. However the conductor put me off the bus right on my doorstep. This kindness was much appreciated. On the following Wednesday when I met Ernie at the class I told him about the long cold wait at the coach station. He was very concerned and promised to accompany me to Spalding to see me on to the Crowland bus if the situation should arise again so late at night.

The weeks went by and I still saw Ernie twice a week. I had no time now to think about writing my life story and abandoned the idea altogether. Every other weekend he came to see me at Crowland and stayed in the guest room which adjoined the flats. This worked out quite satisfactorily. The cost of the guest room was minimal and I cooked the meals. He would arrive on Saturday afternoon and take me out for a meal in the evening. On Sunday we would attend morning service at the Abbey. He returned to Boston on Sunday evening. The alternate weekend I spent with friends in Boston and on Sunday evenings we attended the service at his church, which was Methodist. I found it rather strange at first for I had always attended Church of England. I was struck with the warmth and friendliness of the people at the chapel. I found at first that I knew very few of the hymns. I had been used to Hymns Ancient and Modern or the English Hymnal. I know so many of them by heart. I particularly enjoy the old harvest hymns.

As the weeks passed by Ernie and I were seen out together quite a lot. Some of my London friends were ready with advice for my good and told me that as I had been hurt once they hoped I would think seriously before I made any decision about my future.

117

Of course it was for me alone to make the decision.

In December Ernie suggested we became engaged at Christmas. I think we had the blessing of the family although my sisters were rather apprehensive at first. I felt better after we had met Ernie's son, Jim, and his family. They were most delightful people. There were three grandchildren of whom I am very proud. All have done extremely well.

After Christmas Ernie put in hand the arrangements for modernising his house and making it easy for a blind person to manage. He went through all the inconvenience of workmen about the house during the wintry weather of January and February 1972. For a few weeks I saw very little of him but he walked to the public telephone to phone me every night no matter what the weather was like.

When the work was finished we put in hand the arrangements for an Easter wedding. The date chosen was Easter Monday, 3rd April. We saw each other every weekend and usually on Wednesdays. In March we were invited to Lincoln to spend a week with Jim, Kath, and family. I felt nervous but after the ice had been broken I really enjoyed the visit. The younger grandson, Peter, was only nine years old and was very helpful to me. I can remember playing marbles with him on the hearthrug after chapel on the Sunday evening. Mick, Jim's elder son, spent most of his time studying. We decided on Ernie's grand-daughter, Judith, as bridesmaid.

About a fortnight before the wedding I spent the weekend with my old friend at Lancaster Gate, in London, and did some shopping in Oxford Street. Meanwhile Ernie was spending the weekend with his cousin in Peterborough. He joined me on the train on the way home and saw me on to the Crowland bus at Spalding. That was the last time we went out separately - until Ernie died.

In early March, a month before our wedding, we attended the funeral of my young sister, Lucy, who had died of leukaemia. While she was in hospital she asked to be introduced to Ernie. On a cold Saturday afternoon we walked to the hospital in the snow to visit her. She wished us well and said she was pleased for us. That was the last time we saw her.

A day or so before the wedding I came to stay with my sister in Boston. On Easter Monday it was all very exciting for the children. My two nieces must have a peep at the dress I was going to wear. Just as I had finished dressing I accidentally pulled a thread in the bottom of the dress and the hem came undone. A friend came to the rescue and stitched it up with one eye on the clock. We were still ready in good time. In fact, we were so early we had to drive around for five minutes. Everything from there onwards went extremely well. The flowers were exquisite as the chapel had already been decorated for Easter. The organ music and the singing were really glorious. The sun shone though there was quite a cool breeze. The reception was in the church hall where we met many old friends.

Next day we took my bouquet of spring flowers to an old friend, Olive, who lived in Ingelow Manor and had spent most of her life confined to a wheelchair with arthritis. We must have walked miles that day delivering wedding cake to friends and relatives.

Once again I was leading a full life with all the household cooking etc. I made all our bread for some years. I also made our jams and chutneys, mincemeat, and Christmas cakes. I have found that cooking for two people is much more rewarding than just cooking for oneself. Ernie undertook the cleaning and washing.

We didn't go away for a holiday that first year. We seemed to find plenty to do at home. Every day when possible we went for walks. Ernie had become very involved in the social club. He was particularly active in fund-raising and organising jumble sales and coffee evenings. He had been retired from his work prematurely with glaucoma in both eyes, though one eye was still quite good. At first he found this difficult to accept. However, the little sight he still possessed was a very great asset to us both. I appreciated getting my private letters read to me without having to call in a neighbour. In my opinion not being able to read our own correspondence is a blind person's biggest embarrassment.

How fast the time seemed to fly during our years together. We had reached 1975 and had been married over three years. Ernie had been elected chairman of our social club. He put his heart and soul into organising fund-raising functions. I baked a weekly batch of brown bread and sold it to friends and neighbours. This was so time consuming that I gave it up after two years.

That summer was a fairly hectic one for Ernie. He decorated

the house inside and outside. By this time his sight was deteriorating and this worried him for he liked to see a job done well. It bothered me when he climbed to such heights painting windows, etc. However he was pleased with the completed job, all the more so when people remarked upon the work. The December gales were exceptionally fierce that year and blew several tiles off the roof. He had to employ a tradesman to replace them. This turned out to be rather costly which didn't please him at all. I must say I was relieved that he didn't attempt the work himself.

That autumn he had organised a very successful jumble sale for the social club. It was held in the local boy scouts' headquarters in Castle Street one Saturday afternoon. Friends and family helped to set out the goods in the hall all morning. I remember it well for I had to cook lunch for twelve. At the end of the day everyone was well satisfied, albeit rather tired.

The summer of 1976 proved to be one of the best, and we got out and about quite a lot. Ernie organised a group holiday for the social club. We stayed at Chaucer House, Skegness, a guest house for blind people and friends. The weather was perfect. We played bowls during the morning, went on excursions, mystery tours, shows, walks in the evening, and usually finished off the day with light refreshments at one of the local hotels.

Later on that year Ernie and I visited London. This was his first visit and I was in charge. My friend who lived at Lancaster Gate invited us for lunch. We walked from Paddington to her flat. Much to Ernie's amazement we arrived at the entrance to the flats without losing ourselves. It hadn't changed in any way since I had lived there. After lunch my friend and I showed Ernie around the locality. Unfortunately an afternoon isn't long enough to go very far afield but it gave him a glimpse of one of my old haunts. Going back home in the train he confided that he would not like to live in London at any price. He thought that Boston would take a lot of beating. I was glad that I had been able to let him see that other world in which I had spent so much of my life.

Very soon afterwards Ernie's health began to give concern and he started to think about moving to a council bungalow where the housework wouldn't be so heavy. The stairs were rather steep and he feared for my safety should it become necessary for me to do the cleaning which was his province. His name was already on the housing list for, before he met me, he had decided the house was too large for one person. It was not very long before we were allocated a bungalow in an area of our choice. The old house, which belonged to Ernie's son, sold almost immediately. What a contrast in the household chores in a small bungalow to those in a large house with stairs! When we settled down we were pleased with the change. We were within easy reach of the town and had a small garden which Ernie enjoyed tending.

We had been living in our new abode a few weeks when Ernie experienced what he thought was a severe attack of indigestion. I didn't like the sound of this so we made an appointment to visit his doctor. The walk to the surgery was quite a long one but didn't seem to bother him unduly. The doctor diagnosed angina. He was prescribed the relevant tablets and didn't appear to be very worried. I am afraid it troubled me quite a lot for I had come across this sort of thing previously. I tried to do my best when cooking to leave out those things supposed to be harmful, such as animal fats. I had learned a lot from reading the health section of my woman's magazine which I took in braille each month.

He seemed to be quite well in the summer of 1978 so we decided to take a holiday not too far from home. We picked Skegness again as it was the nearest seaside resort. The holiday was a disappointment for he was quite ill most of the time. We spent sleepless nights but he wouldn't see a doctor. When we returned home we called the doctor who told him that he must rest for ten days. I was asked if I could cope. I was sure I could. The hardest task of all was to get him to stay in bed. He insisted upon sitting at the table for meals because he said it was too much work for me; I argued with him but to no avail. I did manage to take his drinks to him in bed because he didn't know when they were coming. However, he was allowed to get up at the end of the ten days' rest. I think the enforced rest did pay dividends in the long run but I have often wondered since whether he would have been better without that holiday.

At the beginning of 1981 Ernie resigned his position as social club chairman because of his health. It was a very quiet year for us and on the whole things seemed a little easier. We gave up the idea of holidays that year. We often walked in the local park where we spent many enjoyable hours sitting on a bench watching tennis and bowls.

Christmas that year was a very quiet one. The weather was frosty and cold and the windows crusted over with ice. The New Year came in with frost and snow just like a Christmas card.

On Saturday morning, 9th January, Ernie seemed very unwell. I decided to call the doctor who was here within minutes. He left some tablets saying that if there was no improvement I must let them know. We thought he would be better after a sleep. After a brief period, feeling very concerned, I called in a friend who advised me to call the doctor again. It was his regular doctor this time. He did not need to tell me in words. I knew this was his final sleep.

My sister came to stay with me for a fortnight and friends rallied round for a while but the gap which was left would take some filling.

The five years which have elapsed since then have on the whole been rather empty in many respects. On the first occasion when this blow overtook me I had my job and colleagues at work to turn to and after a few years was able to start living again. That was over thirty years ago and the pattern of life is changing all the time. We are caught up in the net, sometimes forced to travel in a direction not of our own choice.

I think it can be said that the patchwork quilt referred to at the beginning of this book is more or less the colour of my life. Of course there have been limitations. Some hurdles I have managed to overcome. On the whole I think life has dealt with me pretty fairly. The story isn't finished yet. Neither is the quilt. Let's hope there are a few more bright patches to add to it.

– * –